Animal Planet®

Staffordshire Bull Terriers

TRACY LIBBY

Staffordshire Bull Terriers
Project Team
Editors: Stephanie Fornino and Heather Russell-Revesz
Copy Editor: Joann Woy
Interior Design: Leah Lococo Ltd. and Stephanie Krautheim
Design Layout: Stephanie Krautheim

T.F.H. Publications
President/CEO: Glen S. Axelrod
Executive Vice President: Mark E. Johnson
Publisher: Christopher T. Reggio
Production Manager: Kathy Bontz

T.F.H. Publications, Inc.
One TFH Plaza
Third and Union Avenues
Neptune City, NJ 07753

Discovery Communications, Inc. Book
Development Team
Maureen Smith, Executive Vice President &
General Manager, Animal Planet
Carol LeBlanc, Vice President, Licensing
Elizabeth Bakacs, Vice President, Creative Services
Caitlin Erb, Licensing Specialist

Printed and bound in China
07 08 09 10 11 1 3 5 7 9 8 6 4 2

Library of Congress Cataloging-in-Publication Data

Libby, Tracy, 1958-
  Staffordshire bull terriers / Tracy Libby.
    p. cm. – (Animal Planet pet care library)
  Includes index.
  ISBN-13: 978-0-7938-3776-2 (alk. paper) 1. Staffordshire bull terrier. I. Title.
  SF429.S85L53 2007
  636.755'9–dc22
                                    2006033041

This book has been published with the intent to provide accurate and authoritative information in regard to the subject matter within. While every precaution has been taken in preparation of this book, the author and publisher expressly disclaim responsibility for any errors, omissions, or adverse effects arising from the use or application of the information contained herein. The techniques and suggestions are used at the reader's discretion and are not to be considered a substitute for veterinary care. If you suspect a medical problem consult your veterinarian.

The Leader In Responsible Animal Care For Over 50 Years!™

www.tfh.com

Table of Contents

Chapter 1

Why I Adore My

Staffordshire Bull Terrier

Who would have thought that nearly 200 years ago, a Bulldog crossed with a terrier would produce one of England's—and eventually America's—most beloved dogs? Today, Staffordshire Bull Terriers, or Staffords as they are affectionately called, have a steadfast and devoted—if not obsessive—following. Breed enthusiasts cite the Stafford's supreme intelligence, courage, loyalty, love of children, welcoming grin, and uncanny ability to ham it up for the camera as some of the breed's most endearing traits.

Weaving Through History

To thoroughly understand the history of the Staffordshire Bull Terrier, one must look back in history—well beyond the Greek, Macedonian, and Roman armies. Of course, doing so would fill an entire book, so in keeping within the scope of this book, let's fast-forward a few centuries. In Germany around the 16th century, during the post-Renaissance era, a breed known as the Bullenbeisser emerged. Experts believe the Bullenbeisser descended from the Molossus-type dog who accompanied Roman soldiers on their way to conquering most of the known world. Butchers allegedly used the *Bullenbeisser*, which translates to "bull biter," to bait, or attack, a tethered bull, grip its nose, and attempt to throw it to the ground. Doing so supposedly inundated the bull's otherwise unpalatable flesh with adrenaline, thereby tenderizing it for consumption.

Around the same time in England, similar Molossus descendents were being used for the same bull-baiting purpose. Over time, both a larger and smaller type of English bull-baiting dog began to emerge, and naturally they both became known as Bulldogs. Of course, back then, these old-style Bulldogs differed greatly from the English Bulldogs we know and love today.

Bull-baiting evolved into a "sport" that attracted large groups of

Top Dog

The Staffordshire Bull Terrier falls in the terrier group in the classifications of both the American Kennel Club (AKC) and the Kennel Club in the United Kingdom. One of the most popular registered breeds in the United Kingdom, Staffords and their owners are quite a common sight on the streets of London, having carved out a special place in the heart of the British dog-owning public.

spectators, but it was eventually outlawed in the early 1800s. In its place, however, other equally cruel blood sports, such as dog fighting, began to flourish. Somewhere along the line, by design or happenstance (no one knows for certain), someone crossed the smaller-type Bulldog with a terrier, producing the popular and notable bull-and-terrier dog. Varying opinions abound about the type of terrier involved, but the now extinct Old English Terrier seems to be the most generally accepted dog. The bull-and-terrier crosses produced a dog who possessed both the strength and tenacity of the Bulldog and the speed and quick reactions of the terrier. These new bull-and-terrier crossbreeds became the top dogs of the sport of dog fighting. However, it wasn't until 1935 that the U.K. Kennel Club recognized the breed that became known as the Staffordshire Bull Terrier.

The popularity of the new crossbreeds spread rapidly, and records indicate that by the mid-1800s, bull-and-terrier crosses had reached the shores of Australia, South Africa, and the United States. In his book *The Staffordshire Bull Terrier Story,* Steve Stone (considered the father of the breed in the United States) writes about a bull-and-terrier being used to hunt wolves in the American West, as well as a 1904 photograph showing Freddie Austerlitz (better known as Fred Astaire) with his bull-and-terrier dog. And you might remember Petey from the popular television series *Our Gang*—a bull-and-terrier with the unforgettable ring around one eye. While many bull-and-terrier dogs continued to be used as fighters, others were treasured family pets, hunting dogs, farm dogs, and cattle dogs. Today's Staffordshire Bull Terrier breed is a descendant of these old Bulldog and terrier crossbreeds.

The Stafford Comes to America

Although the Stafford's unique history and origin remain somewhat elusive in his homeland, the breed's American roots are relatively well documented, thanks to the diligence, perseverance, and stellar record-keeping skills of early breed pioneers, including Steve Stone. While living in Finland in the early 1960s, Stone acquired a Staffordshire Bull Terrier imported from England. Bandits Belle Lettres—"Bella" to her family—became the breed's first representative in that country. Stone fell in love with the breed, and in 1966, he returned to the United States with

Staffords were developed by crossing Bulldogs and terriers.

Why I Adore My Staffordshire Bull Terrier

the intention of founding a Staffordshire Bull Terrier Club.

At that time in the United States, six families owned 14 Staffords—scattered from New York to Chicago to Los Angeles. Stone contacted each of the families and January 14, 1967, was chosen as the founding date of the Staffordshire Bull Terrier Club of the USA (SBTC/USA).

Mr. Stone began importing Staffords from England, and it wasn't long before domestic litters were bred and registered with the SBTC/USA. While the breed began attracting attention and gaining in popularity among breed enthusiasts, the Staffordshire Bull Terrier languished in relative obscurity until the American Kennel Club (AKC) recognized the breed in 1975. Today, Staffordshire Bull Terriers retain their popularity as an all-around family dog and supreme performance dog, competing and excelling in agility, obedience, flyball, and even lure coursing.

The Staffordshire Look

Staffords are frequently mistaken for their cousin, the American Staffordshire Terrier (AmStaff) or a number of other Bully breeds, such as the American Pit Bull Terrier and occasionally the Bull Terrier. Although these Bully breeds all lay claim to the Bulldog as a common ancestor, important mental and physical differences separate one breed from another and contribute to each dog's breed type.

Breed type is described in the Stafford's breed standard, and to the newcomer, it may seem like nothing more than a cluster of strange-sounding words strung together on a piece of paper. However, *breed type* is a breeder's blueprint for success because it describes the "ideal" Stafford—everything from height to weight to color to coat to what he should look like when he is moving. Even if you don't plan to show your dog, it's fun to look at the standard because it

Stubby and Sallie Ann: American War Heroes

Long before the Bulldog became the official mascot of Georgetown University, Stubby, a bull-and-terrier, had the job. However, before his university mascot gig, he was a war hero, serving with the 102nd Infantry Regiment during World War I. During his 18 months on the front lines, Stubby located wounded soldiers, saved his regiment from a mustard gas attack, carried messages under fire, and even captured a German spy. Invited to the White House by Presidents Wilson, Coolidge, and Harding, Stubby also received a gold medal of valor from General Pershing.

Stubby wasn't the first bull-and-terrier to help America's fighting men. Sallie Ann Jarrett, a bull-and-terrier and regimental mascot of the 11th Pennsylvania Volunteers, stood bravely under fire, refusing to leave the wounded soldiers of her regiment during the three-day stand at Gettysburg. She is immortalized in bronze at the foot of the 11th Regiment's Monument at Gettysburg National Military Park.

will help you to understand why your dog looks like he does and what makes him tick. Remember, though, the traits described in this section are based on the "ideal" Stafford, as envisioned by those who invented the breed. Understanding the standard and why fanciers have preserved specific characteristics will lead to a greater appreciation of your Stafford. And although breeders strive to breed quality dogs who measure up to the standard, a dog who isn't "show" quality is no less a trusted and loyal companion.

General Appearance

The first thing you probably notice when you see a Stafford is his remarkable beauty, smooth coat, good muscles, compact size, and the unmistakable Stafford grin that gives him a comical or laughing appearance—as if he's just heard a funny joke. The Stafford's overall look should convey his character and temperament—kind, courageous, highly intelligent, tenacious, and dignified—as well as an appearance of strength and agility. The Stafford should be a balanced blend of "bull" and "terrier."

Size

Weighing in at 28 to 38 pounds (12.7 to 17.3 kg) for males and 24 to 34 pounds (10.9 to 15.5 kg) for females, you might also notice that the Stafford is quite a bit smaller than the American Staffordshire Terrier, which is a much larger and leggier dog—sometimes

Staffordshire Bull Terriers (page 10) *are often mistaken for their cousins, American Staffordshire Terriers* (page 11, left), *or American Pit Bull Terriers* (page 11, right).

twice the size of a Stafford.

Color

The Staffordshire Bull Terrier comes in an assortment of colors and can be red, fawn, white, black, or blue, or any one of the colors with white. He can also be any shade of brindle or any shade of brindle with white.

SENIOR DOG TIP

The Senior Years

Staffordshire Bull Terriers are a pretty healthy breed, with an average lifespan of between 12 and 14 years. Although this might seem like a long time to you, 12 to 14 years is a relatively short time in terms of dog years. Remember, in about 12 years, your Stafford will have grown from a tiny puppy to a senior citizen. Experts say that 1 human year can be equivalent to 7 to 10 dog years.

Head

A Stafford's head is very distinct and wide, with pronounced cheek muscles, a short foreface, black nose, and the breed's unmistakable welcoming grin. When you look at your own Stafford, you should see these characteristics, too. Generally speaking, a Stafford's eyes should be dark, which is a result of the pigment cells in the iris. His ears should be either "rose" ears, which fold backward (like those of his Bulldog ancestors) or half-pricked. Unlike his Bulldog ancestors, who have a pronounced undershot bite, the Stafford's strong teeth should meet in a scissors bite.

Body

Basically, a dog's internal organs—his heart, lungs, kidneys, and liver—perform the same function for every breed. However, the package in which these

internal organs are wrapped differs from breed to breed. A Stafford's body construction, for example, differs greatly from that of, say, a Greyhound who was originally used for hunting large prey and capable of running as fast as the wind. A Stafford's body should be muscular. As a bull-baiting dog, his wide body provided a good center of gravity so that he could not easily be knocked off his feet. Well-sprung ribs provides sufficient room for his heart and lungs, and a level topline helps him to expend energy efficiently. These factors help to define his physique, which provides the shape and substance of the Stafford breed.

Legs and Feet

A Stafford's front legs should be straight and well boned. His hindquarters are well muscled, strong, and when viewed from behind, his back legs should be parallel. Just as you get sore feet, so too does your dog, and sore feet can hinder his ability to walk or run and even make him a bit cranky. His feet are designed to bear the weight of his body, and they should be well padded, which also helps to protect them from rough surfaces, stickers, burrs, and the like.

Tail

Did you know that how your Stafford carries his tail can tell you if he's happy, sad, angry, or even if he's feeling sick? In a relaxed state, your dog should carry his tail at a downward slope, hanging loosely. As he becomes more attentive, his tail will rise, wagging slightly. If he wants to solicit play, his tail will wag furiously. If he perceives a threat, his tail will rise straight up or slightly over his rear. If he's showing submissive behavior, his tail will usually

Why I Adore My Staffordshire Bull Terrier

FAMILY-FRIENDLY TIP

Staffies and Kids— Friends Forever?

They say that a dog is a man's best friend, but it has been written that "a Stafford is a child's best friend." Always eager to get involved, Staffords generally tolerate any amount of roughhousing with a continual wagging of their tail. The AKC breed standard notes the Stafford's "affection for its friends, and children in particular." The British even nicknamed them "nanny dogs" because of their penchant for watching over children. That said, it is never wise to leave babies and small children unattended with any dog, regardless of how trustworthy you think he might be.

be tucked under him and probably wagging nervously.

Memoirs of a Tough Guy

The Stafford's reputation as a purely tough guy is a bit misleading because his stable and trustworthy temperament is one of the breed's most important and enduring characteristics. Often mistaken for an American Pit Bull Terrier, the breed has received its share of adverse publicity, which is inaccurate and unwarranted. His ancestors may have been fighting dogs, but a well-bred Stafford is trustworthy and loyal to a fault.

Exercise Requirements

Staffords are active, agile dogs who require vigorous physical exercise every day, but they should never be allowed to run loose or roam the neighborhood. Their undeserved bad-boy image and mistaken pit bull identity alone are capable of wreaking havoc in many a neighborhood. The breed is known to have disagreements with other dogs and small animals. Adequate physical and mental stimulation will help to prevent many behavioral problems, such as destructive chewing and digging, and that's why a tired Staffordshire Bull Terrier is a good thing!

Friendliness

Although Staffords are a friend to everyone they meet, remember that they can be quite quarrelsome with other canines and small animals (a throwback to their fearless and feisty terrier heritage, no doubt). However, most well-bred and properly socialized and supervised Staffords can and do live harmoniously with other animals.

Intelligence

The Stafford's intelligence is legendary, and no doubt you've observed remarkable brainpower in your Stafford, too. Perhaps he's figured out how to pop the otherwise secure lid on his food container, or he knows precisely when you are returning from work. Maybe he knows that his dog bones are in the third drawer next to the stove or that the presence of a suitcase means that you're leaving for the weekend. Some Staffords learn tricks and commands quickly but become easily bored after a few repetitions. Others have a dogged determination—taking longer to learn a command, but once learned, they never forget. Either way, most Staffords exhibit a remarkable intelligence, which means that they can and do excel at a variety of canine sports. It also means that you must stay one step ahead of these marvelous creatures at all times!

The Stafford's head is very distinct and wide, with that unmistakable welcoming grin.

Watchdog Ability

Seldom territorial, Staffords are not guard dogs, and they are not likely to care if anyone walks off with your family's silverware. They can, however, be fiercely protective of their owners. Stories have been told of Staffords who possess the uncanny ability to decipher "sound" people from those less reputable, and they are equally capable of defending and protecting their family members from dangerous encounters.

While Staffords are a wellspring of affection and comfort, there are important physical and mental requirements associated with owning one. Understanding the breed's history and origin will help you to understand why your Stafford does what he does—in other words, what makes him tick. And as any owner will attest, despite the breed's quirks and idiosyncrasies, life would be much more boring without Staffordshire Bull Terriers.

Chapter 2

The Stuff of
Everyday Life

Endless opportunities to shop are one of the great perks of canine ownership. Not only can you indulge your precious pooch, you can literally shop till you drop! From pet stores and canine boutiques to catalogs and online vendors, countless non-essential accessories will help your Stafford stand out from the pack.

From a practical standpoint, however, there are some canine products that you and your dog simply cannot do without. So before heading to the checkout line, double-check your cart for these doggy must-haves. Leash? Check. Collar and ID tag? Check, check. Crate, exercise pen, and baby gates? Grooming supplies? Check, check, check. And check. You'll also want to be sure that you have dog food, food and water bowls, a bed, and of course, an assortment of training toys and chew toys.

Be savvy and shop around, but don't sacrifice quality for cost. Remember, cost doesn't always equate to quality, and when possible, it is always prudent to invest in good-quality, top-notch products.

Bed

Your Stafford is sure to appreciate a comfy, cozy place to rest his head, not to mention his weary bones, after a fun-filled day of playing, training, and all that goes into being a dog! However, prudence dictates holding off on the expensive designer model until he is well beyond the chewing stage. Puppies chew, and a tenacious chewer can turn a posh canine bed into worthless confetti in the few minutes it takes you to answer the telephone. A large blanket or towel folded over several times or a cozy fleece pad placed in his crate or exercise pen will do the job for the first few months.

Once he is through the chewing stage, choose a bed that is size-appropriate for your dog. Available in

a variety of materials, colors, shapes, and sizes, dog beds are frequently filled with down, cotton, poly blends, or memory foam. Other are filled with cedar chips for odor and insect control. Most have removable fleece or cotton covers that are easily cleaned in the washing machine and therefore less likely to develop that distinctive doggy smell.

During the housetraining stage, your Stafford should sleep in his crate, which will prevent accidents. Crate pads come in an assortment of materials, from cotton to plush sheepskin. Be sure that the crate pad you choose is washable, because if he has an accident, you'll need to toss it in the washing machine.

Dog Duty

Your Stafford can't take care of himself, so you and your family must set up a schedule to ensure his feeding, pottying, training, exercise/playtime, grooming, and snuggling needs are met on a regular daily basis. Post a schedule, and choose appropriate family members to help out.

Collar

You can have a lot of fun indulging your own sense of style with your dog's collar, but

Puppies grow quickly, so check your dog's collar regularly to ensure a proper fit.

remember, it serves an important function, so never sacrifice quality and comfort for style. A collar holds your dog's license and ID tag, which is his ticket home should he become lost.

Puppies grow quickly, so check his collar regularly to ensure a proper fit, replacing it as he grows bigger and stronger. Invest in a good-quality, durable, and properly sized and weighted collar. Good-quality leather collars are more expensive than nylon but well worth the investment for adult dogs because they are softer yet sturdier. Given the right care, they will last a lifetime.

Several types of collars work by putting pressure on your dog's neck and throat, like choke chains, prong collars, or martingale collars. Although it may be tempting to use these devices on a strong dog like the Staffordshire Bull Terrier, these collars are best left to professionals.

Crate

A crate provides comfort and security for your Stafford, a cozy den for sleeping, and a safe spot to retreat from the poking, prodding fingers of toddlers and the often chaotic and noisy world of humans. Crates also are ideal for traveling, housetraining, and feeding.

Purchase a crate that is big enough for your Stafford when he is full grown. Ideally, it should be big enough for an adult Stafford to stand up, turn around, and stretch out in while lying down. If the crate is too big, though, it defeats the purpose of providing the security of a den. During the housetraining stage, a crate that is too large allows a puppy to use one end for sleeping and the other end as a bathroom, which of course defeats its usefulness as a housetraining tool. However, if it is too small, your Stafford will be cramped and uncomfortable, and this is neither fair nor humane. Some crates come equipped with a divider panel that allows you to adjust the crate space accordingly. This type of crate can take your Stafford from the puppy stage through housetraining and into adulthood without the expense of

17

A crate provides comfort and security for your Stafford.

purchasing multiple different-sized crates.

Crates and kennels come in a variety of sizes and materials, which offer their own advantages. Folding wire crates are easy to transport between car and house and provide good visibility and air circulation, keeping your pooch cool when temperatures are high. Other crate types include heavy-duty, high-impact plastic kennels that meet requirements for airline travel. Nylon crates are lightweight and portable, but they may not be the ideal choice for the tenacious chewer.

A good-quality crate will last a lifetime, and the benefits definitely make it well worth the cost when one considers the alternative of replacing damaged carpet and furniture 6 months down the road.

Food and Water Bowls

No doubt your dog considers his food bowl the most important item on your list of must-have supplies. After all, mealtimes are some of a dog's best times, and you want to be sure that your puppy or dog has bowls for both food and water. From custom-painted ceramic ware to stainless steel to durable plastic bowls, the selection is seemingly endless. You will need two bowls: one for water and one for food.

Stainless Steel
Ideally, you should focus on stainless steel, which is durable, virtually nondestructible, easily sanitized and—perhaps most important—dishwater safe. Some come with rubber bases to keep them from sliding on the floor.

Plastic
Plastic bowls are inexpensive, but they are not the best choice for the tenacious chewer who could ingest or choke on shredded pieces. Also, plastic is not as easily sanitized as stainless steel and can harbor bacteria.

Ceramic

Ceramic bowls are beautiful and decorative, but they are breakable and usually expensive. If you choose this route, be sure that the ceramic is finished with a nontoxic glaze and is dishwasher safe.

Grooming Tools

Keeping your Stafford looking and feeling good requires the right tools. The must-have supplies for general grooming include a soft bristle brush, flat soft slicker brush, grooming glove (also known as a hound's glove) and rubber curry comb, or both. You also need a good-quality shampoo and conditioner designed specifically for dogs. Nail clippers designed specifically for dogs, styptic powder (in case you accidentally nip the quick), ear cleaner and cotton swabs for cleaning the ears, and a doggy toothbrush and toothpaste designed for dogs should be included in your mosaic of grooming paraphernalia, too.

An assortment of grooming cases and containers are available, and I highly recommend that you buy one. It need not be fancy, and a small plastic bin or canvas tote works equally well. The key is organization and accessibility, and a tote or container provides both.

Identification

Two common types of identification are ID tags and microchips. Ideally, your dog should have both.

ID Tags

Your Stafford must have an ID tag that includes, at the minimum, your name and telephone number. These tags are relatively inexpensive and well worth the investment because they are your

19

The Expert Knows

Licensing Your Stafford

Most county and state laws require that your Stafford be licensed once he reaches the age of 6 months or once he has his permanent canine teeth. License fees vary from area to area, but most are nominal and well worth the investment because a dog license tells everyone that your Stafford is not homeless.

To apply for a license, contact your local animal control agency for proper paperwork. You may even be able to apply online. The form will ask for your name, address, and telephone number, as well as your pet's name, breed, sex, age, microchip number (if any), and whether your pet has been neutered. You may need to supply a copy of your dog's rabies vaccination certificate and sterilization certificate.

The Stuff of Everyday Life

FAMILY-FRIENDLY TIP

Childhood Chores

Kids and canines seem to go hand in hand, and Staffords are the best and most delightful of childhood cohorts. But young children should not be the sole caretakers of dogs because they quickly lose interest in things, and teenagers are, well, busy being teenagers. Children can, however, learn to be responsible when you delegate specific dog-related chores and shared chores, such as helping with grooming, feeding, watering, and walking the dog. In the process, your Stafford is well cared for and your child learns compassion and respect. She will learn that the dog needs water when he's thirsty, food when he's hungry, a bath when he's dirty, a clean bed to sleep on, and plenty of love.

dog's ticket home should he become lost or separated from you. ID tags are readily available and can be ordered from your veterinarian, pet stores, catalogs, and online vendors. Available in a variety of shapes, sizes, colors, and materials, they easily attach to your dog's buckle collar with an S-clip or split ring. Some ID tags attach directly to the collar, not unlike a nameplate

on a horse's halter. Unfortunately, they can also become lost if they fall off. Some tags fade, making the engraving difficult, if not impossible, to read.

Microchips

Fortunately, a more permanent method of identification is available—the microchip. A microchip is a tiny rice-sized silicon chip that is painlessly and permanently inserted under your Stafford's skin, usually between the shoulder blades, by a veterinarian. The microchip contains an unalterable identification number that is recorded on a central database along with your name, address, and telephone number. If your wayward dog turns up at a veterinarian's clinic or humane society, his microchip can be scanned, and within mere seconds, his identification number will pop up on the hand-held scanner. The ID number is then cross-referenced with your contact information. Several state and national registries are available for registering and storing your contact information. As with ID tags, you'll want to be sure this information is kept current.

Leash

Like collars, leashes are an essential piece of equipment for every dog owner. They come in a variety of choices, but when all is said and done, choosing a leash is usually a matter of preference.

Nylon Leashes

Nylon leashes are lightweight and relatively inexpensive. They work great

Leashes are an essential piece of equipment for every dog owner. (top) A harness takes the pressure off a dog's trachea. (right)

for puppies but are not always the best choice for strong adult dogs because they are hard on your hands and can slice your finger to the bone should your Stafford give a good lunge or pull.

Leather Leashes
Leather leashes are more expensive than nylon but well worth the investment because they are softer on your hands. That's important, because you'll be using the leash a lot, and the more you use it, the softer and more pliable it becomes.

Retractable Leads
Retractable leads are designed to extend and retract at the touch of a button, allowing your Stafford plenty of distance on walks without carrying a long line that can get tangled, dragged through the mud, or wrapped around bushes. A retractable lead that extends to 16 feet (4.9 m) is ideal. If you go this route, be sure to invest in a good-quality retractable lead designed specifically for strong Stafford-type dogs.

Harnesses
A harness is another option for your Stafford. It will not keep your dog from pulling, but it will take the pressure off his trachea, because the harness goes around his body, not his neck. A variety of models are available in different shapes, sizes, and materials. Seek professional advice to fit your Stafford correctly with a harness and prevent chafing.

Toys
Staffords, like all dogs, love to chew. They *need* to chew—especially puppies, who will experience teething

SENIOR DOG TIP

Age Defying

Adopting an older dog is a wonderful idea, and older dogs can make great pets. However, because they are older, they often have quirks and behaviors that you never fully understand, and they may take time to adjust to their new surroundings. Here are a few tips to help an older dog adjust to his new home and make his homecoming a happy and positive one:

1. Introduce him slowly to children, other pets, grooming, and his new home. Show him around the house, yard, and potty area.
2. Stay with him. Let him know you're around. Keep him safe, and reassure him that he is safe.
3. Feed him a quality diet.
4. Give him plenty of exercise, but don't overdo it.
5. Give him a comfy bed of his own. Unless you're 100 percent certain he's housetrained, consider crate training him. Place the crate next to your bed so that he can feel secure if he wakes up at night.
6. Be patient. Never scold or hit him. Give him time to adjust to his new surroundings.

as their baby teeth erupt and fall out. Toys and chewies are an essential item, and you can never have too many when you own a Stafford!

A seemingly endless selection of specially designed dog toys is available, and you and your Stafford can have a lot of fun selecting favorites. Your healthiest and most long-lasting selections will be toys made for your Stafford's body type and chewing power. Chews and toys designed for a Yorkshire Terrier, for example, are too small for your Staffordshire and could present a choking hazard.

Choose toys that are strong, durable, and well made, such as hard nylon and rubber toys, designed for real gnawing and gashing. They exercise your dog's teeth and gums, promoting oral health while relieving the need to chew.

Cute squeaky toys are adorable and usually irresistible but may not be the best selection for your Stafford. A tenacious puppy (or adult dog) will chew right through the material and may swallow the stuffing or squeaker, which could become lodged in his throat.

Give your dog appropriate toys and chewies to play with.

Edible chews and toys for dogs provide nutritional enhancement or breath fresheners. Most are strong enough for your Stafford to get a good chew before breaking into tiny bits that can be eaten. These should not be substitutes for the more long-lasting chew toys, but they make an enjoyable break for your dog.

Toys that satisfy your Stafford's need to chew while simultaneously stimulating his mind—such as treat-filled hard rubber toys—are equally important.

Toys are a lot of fun, as well as a necessity, but don't go overboard. Stash a few toys, and then surprise him with a new one when he least expects it. Also, save a few special toys in reserve, such as a flying disc or rope tug, for interactive play between you and your dog.

X-Pens and Baby Gates

Exercise pens and baby gates corral curious puppies, keep them away from household hazards, and prevent them from developing bad habits, such as peeing from one end of the house to the other, chewing furniture, and ransacking trash cans. Exercise pens are ideal anywhere you need a temporary kennel area, such as in the kitchen, family room, or backyard.

When strategically placed, baby gates give your Stafford a bit more freedom indoors without allowing him free run of the house. Just like baby gates for toddlers, they easily attach to door frames, confining your dog to one room or a part of the house.

Once you've purchased the basic necessities, your Stafford will be ready to eat, sleep, and step out in style. Remember, shopping for your Stafford is an ongoing process—just like shopping for toddlers and teenagers! Collars, leashes, bowls, and beds will need to be replaced at least once or twice over the course of your Stafford's life.

Chapter 3

Good Eating

The old adage "You are what you eat" applies to your Staffordshire Bull Terrier just as much as it applies to you. A good-quality diet will give him the energy he needs to get through the day. What is good for you, however, is not always good for your dog. That's why you must feed him a good quality, well-balanced diet specifically designed for dogs. Proper nutrition can help prevent disease, promote healthy skin and coat, and provide your Stafford with optimum health and longevity.

Many premium brand foods are available. However, the most expensive may not be the best, and rarely are the least expensive foods of good quality. Your veterinarian can help you choose a good-quality premium food that fits your budget and is right for your Stafford.

Nutrition Know-How

Your Stafford's diet is likely to change several times over the course of his lifetime. However, the nuts and bolts of canine nutrition remain the same. There are six basic elements of nutrition: carbohydrates, fats, minerals, proteins, vitamins, and water.

Carbohydrates

Dogs are omnivorous animals, meaning they eat both animal and vegetable foods, and they get most of their energy from carbohydrates. Carbohydrates fuel your Stafford's body, giving him the energy he needs to chase a ball or tussle with his canine buddies.

Soluble carbohydrates consist mainly of starches and sugars, and are easily digested. They are introduced in your Stafford's diet primarily through cereal grains, such as rice, wheat, corn, barley, and oats. Carbs are good, but if your Stafford doesn't get enough exercise to burn all those carbohydrates, he can become overweight.

Insoluble carbohydrates, better known as *fiber*, come primarily from the cell walls of plants and grains, such as corn, soybean hulls, beet pulp, bran, peanut hulls, and pectin. Fiber does not provide your Stafford with energy, but it is important, especially for improved bowel function.

Fats

Fats make dog food taste good so that your Stafford will eat it, but they also play an important nutritional role. Like carbohydrates, fats and oils are a source of food energy for your Stafford. Fats also help to metabolize fat-soluble vitamins, such as vitamins A, D, K, and E, keeping your Stafford's coat and skin healthy and shiny.

They also contain more than twice the calories of carbohydrates and proteins, so you must keep an eye on how much fat your dog is eating. Too much fat will cause him to gain weight, which is not good for his health or his waistline. If your Stafford is overweight,

Proper nutrition can help prevent disease.

How to Read the Label

Reading dog food labels is no different from reading the labels on your own food, although both can be equally tricky to decipher. Here are the basics: Labels have two main parts—the main display panel and the information panel (known as the statutory statement in Europe).

The main display panel is really about marketing—making the product look attractive to you. The label must have a product name, a net weight, and a designator that says that the product is intended for animals as opposed to humans.

The information panel includes a list of ingredients in descending order by weight. This can be a bit misleading, because it doesn't tell you anything about the quality of the ingredients or their nutritional value. For example, meat may be listed first but only because its high moisture content makes it the heaviest. In reality, the grain might contribute a greater percentage of the protein in the finished product.

The information panel also includes a guaranteed analysis that breaks down by percentage what nutrients are in the food. It lists minimum levels of crude protein and crude fat and maximum levels of crude fiber and moisture. Again, this can be misleading because "21 percent protein" doesn't tell you anything about the quality, nutritional value, or digestibility of the protein.

The label also states whether the food is intended for puppies, adults, seniors, or all life stages, and whether the food is intended to be a complementary product or if it provides complete balanced nutrition for a dog, as established by the nutrient guidelines of the Association of American Feed Control Officials (AFFCO).

Feeding instructions and guidelines on how much and how often you should feed your Stafford are also detailed on the information panel. These are merely guidelines—you may need to tweak the amount depending on the age, weight, and activity level of your dog.

Experienced dog fanciers often have trouble making heads or tails of dog food labels, so don't feel discouraged if you're feeling confused, too. When in doubt, your veterinarian can help you select an appropriate food, as well as determine how much and how often to feed your Stafford

he may be getting too much fat or too little exercise, or both.

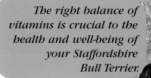
The right balance of vitamins is crucial to the health and well-being of your Staffordshire Bull Terrier.

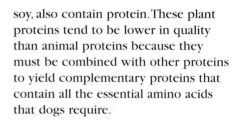

Minerals

Minerals are important because they help regulate your Stafford's complex body systems. They work with vitamins and enzymes to help build strong bones and teeth, transport oxygen in the blood, and help your dog's muscles and nerves to function properly. Minerals, like other components of canine nutrition, must be balanced for good health.

Proteins

Chicken, beef, lamb, and turkey are the most common forms of protein and should be the first ingredients listed on dog food packages. Other sources include fish, fish meal, liver, milk, milk products, and eggs.

If you remember high school biology, proteins are compounds of carbon, hydrogen, oxygen, and nitrogen atoms arranged into a string of amino acids—much like the pearls on a necklace. Amino acids build vital proteins that, in turn, build strong muscles, ligaments, organs, bones, teeth, and coat. Not all proteins are created equal, however. Eggs are considered the highest in protein quality, followed by fish meal, milk, and beef. These are complete proteins. Some products, such as rice, wheat, corn, barley, and soy, also contain protein. These plant proteins tend to be lower in quality than animal proteins because they must be combined with other proteins to yield complementary proteins that contain all the essential amino acids that dogs require.

Vitamins

Your Stafford's body does not get energy from vitamins, but like minerals, they are important because they help to fight disease, absorb minerals, regulate metabolism, and help your Stafford to grow and function normally.

Interestingly, dogs can make vitamin C from glucose, so they don't need to acquire it in their diet. All other water-soluble vitamins, however, must be replenished on a daily basis through the diet. Fat-soluble vitamins (A, D, E, and K) are absorbed and stored in the body's liver and fatty tissues. The right balance of vitamins is crucial to the health and well-being of your Staffordshire Bull Terrier.

Water

Water is the single most important nutrient needed to sustain your four-legged friend's health. Water regulates your dog's temperature, supports metabolic reactions, allows blood to carry vital nutritional materials to cells, and removes waste products from your dog's system.

The amount of water your dog needs daily will vary depending on growth, stress, environment, weather temperature, activity, and age. If he eats primarily dry food, he'll need plenty of water to wash it down and aid in digestion. A dog's water requirement also increases when he expends energy working, exercising, playing, or training because dogs cool themselves by panting, which is accomplished largely by the evaporation of water.

Provide your Stafford with access to an abundant supply of fresh, cool drinking water at all times. If you have less than desirable city water, consider a filtration system or purchase bottled water.

Commercial Foods

Now that you are armed with the basics of canine nutrition, let's take a look at the different commercial meal options available. It's worth noting that no single dog food is "best." You may need to try a few to see what works best for your dog. Grocery stores, feed stores, and pet stores are the most convenient and popular locations for purchasing dog food. Veterinary offices also sell foods, and this is a good option, especially for dogs who

SENIOR DOG TIP

Feeding the Senior Dog

As Staffords age, they can feel the aches and pains of sore muscles, and sometimes they're not as active as they used to be, which means they'll need fewer calories. Otherwise, they are likely to start packing on some extra pounds (kg). Other dogs lose interest in their food, and that can cause them to lose a lot of weight.

Senior dogs often develop conditions associated with old age, including kidney problems, which means you may need to switch to a food lower in protein to help lower the workload of your dog's kidneys. Missing or worn teeth and dental disease are also common in older dogs, and that can make chewing hard kibble difficult. Try soaking his food in water to soften it, or switch to a smaller, bite-size kibble.

Your veterinarian is your best bet when it comes to feeding and keeping your Stafford healthy during his golden years.

require special diets, such as senior or overweight dogs or dogs with allergies.

Commercial foods are undoubtedly the most convenient foods to buy, store,

Good Eating

and use. The three most common types are dry, semi-moist, and canned.

Dry Food (Kibble)

By far the most convenient method for buying, storing, and feeding your Stafford, high-quality premium dry foods tend to have high caloric density and good digestibility, meaning lower amounts per serving need to be consumed. Refrigeration is not necessary, and the shelf life for dry food is around 12 months. Dry foods contain a high percentage of carbohydrates in the form of grain. They may improve dental hygiene through chewing and grinding, although this is highly debatable among experts. They do, however, provide some exercise for your Stafford's mouth and help to satisfy a puppy's need to chew.

Semi-Moist Foods

Semi-moist foods are yummy to most dogs because they are high in moisture and sugar. Too much sugar, however, may cause spikes in blood sugar levels and contribute to obesity— neither of which are good for your Stafford. Generally marketed in sealed and resealable pouches, semi-moist foods come in all shapes and sizes—the most common being hamburger-type patties. Ingredients can include fresh or frozen animal tissues, cereal grains, fats, and simple sugar. Semi-moist foods lack the unmistakable (and frequently offensive) smell of some canned foods, but they may contain a number of chemicals and artificial colors. Be sure to read the label and check the food's nutritional content before feeding.

Canned Food

Canned foods are extremely appealing to dogs because they are chock full of chunky meats and delectable gravies. And they smell good, too! Okay, maybe not to you, but to your Stafford, they smell wonderful.

Canned foods have a high water content—up to 75 percent—with little grain, which makes the food more palatable than dry food. Available in an endless selection of flavors, combinations, and recipes, canned foods are highly digestible and contain a higher meat protein level than dry foods.

Canned food does have a few

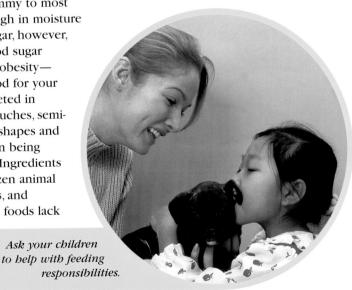

Ask your children to help with feeding responsibilities.

drawbacks, though. For starters, it's generally more expensive than dry foods. The higher water content means it has fewer nutrients than dry foods, so dogs must eat more to satisfy their energy and nutrient needs. This might not be a problem for, say, a Yorkshire Terrier owner, but it might prove too costly when it comes to feeding a Staffordshire Bull Terrier. Canned foods also don't provide abrasion from chewing, which may allow faster plaque and tartar buildup on teeth. It can cause diarrhea in some dogs. Once opened, it is susceptible to spoilage, and leftovers must be refrigerated.

Non-Commercial Diets

Although commercial diets provide your dog with a balanced, no-fuss diet, you may opt to feed a homemade diet or raw diet. Keep in mind that when you choose to feed a raw or homemade diet, you assume full responsibility for the nutritional status of your Stafford. Before jumping in, consider these factors:

- Preparing a homemade or raw diet is time consuming and labor intensive. Will you have the time or energy to cook Fido's dinner after a long day at the office? When the kids are sick? When the in-laws are visiting?

- Do you have the space to store the

The Expert Knows

Supplements

Supplements are considered anything given in addition to your dog's food. In most cases, if you are feeding a professional-quality diet that is complete and well balanced, supplementing is not required or recommended because these diets typically contain all the vitamins and minerals your Stafford needs to stay healthy. If you still feel that you'd like to enhance your dog's diet with a multi-vitamin or mineral supplement, consult your veterinarian. If you are feeding a homemade diet, supplements may be necessary to ensure that your Stafford is getting his daily minimum requirements of vitamins and minerals. A veterinarian or veterinary nutritionist can help you find the right sources and the correct dosage.

ingredients? Raw meats do not have preservatives, so they will need to be stored in the refrigerator or freezer.

- Organic ingredients are more expensive and can be difficult to find. Are you willing to pay the extra money?

- Canine nutrition is complicated. Do you know enough to ensure that your Stafford is getting complete and balanced levels of nutrients, including vitamins and minerals, on a regular basis?

- If you choose this route, it is prudent to consult with a

Good Eating

veterinarian or certified veterinary nutritionist before proceeding.

Now, let's take a look at the pros and cons of both raw and homemade diets.

Raw Diets

Raw diets are just that—raw meat and bones that you feed your Stafford. Often referred to as the BARF (Bones and Raw Food) plan, it is not difficult to find proponents and opponents on both sides of this controversial diet. Essentially, some people believe that drying, freezing, heating, or canning robs food of its nutritional components. They believe that raw meat and bones compose a more suitable diet for dogs. Some believe the diet improves their dogs' skin, coat, and teeth, and allows their pets to live longer and have healthier lives and better immune systems.

Opponents caution against bacterial infections, parasites, and food-borne illnesses for both dogs and humans when handling and eating raw foods, such as raw meat, poultry, eggs, and unprocessed milk. Also, dogs who eat raw bones are susceptible to choking or stomach damage.

Some manufacturers are now selling raw diets in pet and specialty stores. Usually found in the freezer section, these diets are individually packaged to make feeding simple.

Homemade Diets

Homemade diets are meals made at home from scratch. Owners who choose this route want to feed natural

Puppies have different nutritional requirements.

foods free of preservatives, additives, and who knows what else. Owners can customize their dogs' diet by providing a daily mixture of fresh meat, chicken, fish, vegetables, and if they choose, commercial kibble. While not impossible, these diets are generally time consuming, labor intensive, and complicated. Too much or too little, or the wrong combinations of nutrients or supplements, can be harmful to your dog.

Feeding Requirements

Puppies and adult dogs have different eating habits, as well as different nutritional and caloric requirements. Puppies spend a significant part of their day playing, which requires a lot of calories. Their bodies grow rapidly, and their systems are busy building strong muscles, bones, and vital organs and establishing a resistance to disease. As a result, for the first 12 months of your puppy's life, he needs a specially formulated growth food that is designed exclusively for these greater energy and nutritional needs. A growing puppy needs about twice as many calories per 2.2 pounds (1 kg) of body weight as an adult Stafford.

Because puppies have small stomachs, they also must be fed smaller amounts of food three or four times a day until they are about 6 months old. From 6 months to 1 year of age and thereafter, you should feed your Stafford two times a day—once in the morning and again in the evening. Again, these feeding schedules are guidelines, and they will differ slightly from dog to dog.

Once you have the feeding schedule down pat, you'll need to feed the correct amount. This can be a bit tricky because puppy growth rates and appetites are primarily dictated by genetics and vary from puppy to puppy. The feeding guidelines on puppy foods will help you establish a starting point. However, many dog food manufacturers are overly generous with their proportions. Your veterinarian is your best bet for determining the proper amount to feed.

Scheduled Feeding Versus Free Feeding

Feeding your puppy (or adult dog) at regular times is very important. It is the essence of scheduled feeding. Pick up whatever food is left after 15 minutes, and if necessary, refrigerate or throw away perishable leftovers to prevent

FAMILY-FRIENDLY TIP

Feeding Chores

Kids can learn a lot about responsibility by helping out with canine chores. They learn their dog needs food when he's hungry, water when he's thirsty, a bath when he's dirty, and a soft bed when he's tired. Kids—especially the younger ones—are always eager to help out, and you can decide at what age and how much responsibility to give your child.

Here are some ways in which your child can be included in day-to-day dog chores:

- Make a contract with her about her canine responsibilities and chores.
- Post a roster or chores chart for your child outlining the dog's feeding and potty times. Have her sound the alarm at the designated feeding times, and check off each chore as it's completed.
- Let your child be in charge of the food bowl. It will be her job to get it out, fill it, clean it, and put it away.
- Let your child measure out the correct amount of food and pour it in the dog bowl.
- Put your child in charge of emptying, cleaning, and refilling Fido's water bowl at least twice a day.

33

Feeding your Stafford is serious business. How much you feed, the type of food, and when you feed will vary depending on your dog's activity level, metabolism, and life stage. Puppies generally require more protein than adult dogs. Some senior dogs remain physically active at 10 years and can continue eating adult maintenance rather than a senior food. This chart is a guideline to help you get started. However, your veterinarian is your best bet when determining how much and what type of food to feed.

Age	Times per day	Amount	Best food
Puppies (8 weeks to 6 months of age)	three times per day (morning, afternoon, and evening); pick up any uneaten food after 15 minutes	approximately ½ cup (118.3 ml) per feeding, although this varies from puppy to puppy, and according to the type of food being fed	dry kibble; designed for growth; high in protein
Adolescents (6 months to 12 months old)	two times per day (morning and evening); pick up any uneaten food after 15 minutes	approximately ½ to 1 cup (118.3 to 237.6 ml) per feeding, depending on your dog's activity level and the type of food being fed	dry kibble; designed for growth; high in protein
Active Adults (those who exercise one or more hours per day)	two times per day (morning and evening); pick up any uneaten food after 15 minutes	approximately ½ to 1 cup (118.3 to 237.6 ml) per feeding. Varies depending on the dog and the type of food being fed	dry kibble designed for adult or active dogs
Sedentary Adults (seniors dogs or those who get no daily exercise)	two times per day (morning and evening); pick up any uneaten food after 15 minutes	approximately 2/3 to 1 cup (157.7 to 237.6 ml) per feeding, depending on the dog and type of food being fed	dry kibble; reduced calorie or adult maintenance
Seniors (older than 8 years)	two times per day (morning and evening); pick up any uneaten food after 15 minutes	2/3 to 1 cup (157.7 to 237.6 ml) per feeding, depending on the dog and type of food being fed	dry kibble; adult maintenance or senior food with more fiber

spoilage. Scheduled feedings allow you to monitor your puppy's food intake and help establish a regular routine of eating and eliminating: What goes in on a regular basis comes out on a regular basis. Designated feeding times also help with the bonding process and help to prevent obesity in your puppy.

Free feeding involves putting your dog's food out, leaving it all day, and allowing him to eat at his leisure. Problems arise with this method because it does not establish a set schedule for feeding and eliminating. Also, if you have multiple dogs, you will not know for certain if all of them are receiving their share of the food. More important, even the best of friends have been known to squabble over food bowls.

Obesity

Some owners think that if they can feel their Stafford's ribs, he's too thin. Not so! Your Stafford should be fit and lean—not too skinny, but not too fat. Unfortunately, as more and more owners pack on extra pounds (kg), so too do their dogs. Staffords who eat too much at mealtime, free feed, or enjoy too many tasty tidbits end up consuming too many calories. Simple mathematics will tell you that too many calories consumed and too few calories burned result in an overweight dog.

How can you help your Stafford fight the battle of the bulge? If your dog is packing on the pounds (kg), the first step is a trip to the veterinarian's office for an examination to assess his overall health and medical condition. A veterinarian can advise you on sensible and healthy ways to reduce your dog's weight. This might include increasing his daily exercise, such as a brisk walk twice a day, swimming, or a daily game of fetch and retrieve. You might need to decrease the amount of food you're feeding him and replace high-calorie snacks with low-fat, low-salt treats. Your veterinarian may even recommend a "light" formula dog food.

You are responsible for your Stafford's nutritional well-being, and while it may seem a daunting task, there are plenty of experts, including veterinarians, canine nutritionists, and dog food representatives, who are willing to share their expertise. So when in doubt, don't be shy about asking questions— because the more informed you are about nutrition, the better off your Staffordshire Bull Terrier will be.

Leaving food out all day might mean that your Stafford has to share!

Chapter 4

Looking Good

The Stafford's short, relatively care-free coat may be one of the many perks that drew you to this remarkable breed. But don't let his good looks deceive you. Keeping that smooth coat in tip-top shape takes some work. You can expect daily, weekly, and semi-monthly grooming rituals to keep his skin, coat, ears, eyes, and nails in first-rate condition.

Responsible breeders spend countless hours handling, touching, and cuddling with their puppies. They check their teeth, eyes, ears, and count their toes—all of which teach the puppy to accept being handled and eventually groomed. By the time your Stafford was 8 weeks old and ready for his new home, he was (hopefully!) used to being handled regularly.

Most dogs love to be groomed, which makes this necessary chore a great way to spend quality time with your Stafford while simultaneously building a strong and mutually trusting human–canine relationship. A puppy who is exposed to positive and delightful grooming experiences grows into an adult dog who takes pleasure in this regular routine.

A quick brushing keeps your puppy looking good and gets him used to grooming.

Getting Accustomed to Grooming

It is best to start grooming practices right away, while your Stafford is young and still receptive to new experiences. Few things are as frustrating as trying to wrestle down a 30-pound (13.6-kg) Stafford who hates to be groomed. If grooming is new to your Stafford, don't despair. Like anything else, start slowly and progress at a rate suitable for the age and mental maturity of your dog.

A grooming table makes the necessary task easier, but any sturdy surface, such as a bench or crate top covered with a non-skid, non-slip surface, is sufficient. Sitting or kneeling on the floor with your Stafford works in a pinch, too. In addition, it is prudent to have all the grooming tools out and within easy reach *before* you start grooming. You never want to turn your back or leave your Stafford on a grooming table unattended. A young dog can easily be injured should he fall or jump.

Puppies have limited attention spans, so do not expect your Stafford pup to stand still for extended periods of time. In the beginning, you want progress—not perfection. Your goal is for him to stand still for a few seconds while you praise him. Harsh handling during these learning stages will only build resentment toward the necessary chore. Progress to the point at which your puppy accepts having his body stroked with your hands, then gently, slowly, and calmly brush him all over. In the beginning, your Stafford may be frightened, nervous, or unsure. Patience and kind handling will help to build his confidence and teach him to accept and enjoy the grooming process. Encourage good behavior by rewarding him with yummy treats and calm praise while he is standing or sitting still.

Grooming Checklist

To keep your Stafford looking and feeling good—and to make your job much easier—you need the right tools. Countless grooming tools are available, but the must-have supplies are pretty basic and can be found at most pet supply stores or online. Invest in good-quality grooming supplies. They cost a bit more, but when properly cared for, they last a lifetime. Here's what you'll need for general grooming:

- **Shampoo and Conditioner.** Choose a shampoo-based rather than detergent-based shampoo, which is gentler on your dog's skin and coat—not to mention your hands! Some shampoos are all-purpose. Others contain oatmeal, lavender, citrus, aloe vera, and other therapeutic ingredients. An all-purpose conditioner will help to restore natural moisture and oil to his skin.
- **Brushes and Grooming Gloves.** For daily brushings, choose a soft bristle brush; a soft, flat slicker brush; and a grooming glove (also known as a hound's glove) or rubber curry comb, or both.
- **Chamois.** A chamois, made specifically for dogs, is great for quick rubdowns and enhancing a coat's natural shine.
- **Nail Clippers.** Invest in a good-quality nail clipper designed specifically for dogs. The most popular styles are the classic pliers style and the guillotine model. Breeders, groomers, and veterinarians have their preferences, and you'll be the best judge as to what works best for you and your dog.
- **Styptic Powder.** Styptic powder stops the flow of blood during those unfortunate and unexpected nail-trimming accidents.

Healthful Habits

Staffords can easily be groomed at home, and doing so on a regular basis allows you to check his entire body for lumps, bumps, cuts, rashes, dry skin, fleas, ticks, stickers, and the like. Check his feet for cuts, torn pads, or broken nails, and examine his mouth for tartar, damaged teeth, or discolored gums. Regular grooming improves your Stafford's appearance and disposition, making him the envy of the neighborhood—not to mention the most handsome dog on the block!

- **Ear Cleaning Solution and Cotton Balls.** Cotton balls are great for cleaning the leather flap of your dog's ear and around his eyes.
- **Toothbrush and Toothpaste.** Always use toothpaste designed specifically for dogs. Never use human toothpaste, which can make your dog sick. Choose a size-appropriate toothbrush for your dog. What works for a Yorkshire Terrier will be too small for your Staffordshire Bull Terrier.

You can use a rubber curry comb to brush your Stafford.

Coat and Skin Care

Wash and wear and *drip dry* are frequently used to describe the Stafford's relatively maintenance-free coat. A Stafford's coat is smooth and beautiful, and although it requires minimum care as compared to, say, a Golden Retriever, keeping it in tip-top shape requires regular care.

Brushing

Ideally, you should run a soft bristle brush over your Stafford's entire body once a day. At the very minimum, he needs a thorough brushing on a weekly basis. Despite their seemingly carefree appearance, Staffords do shed—more than one might think. The amount of shedding varies according to the dog, the season, and climatic conditions. Regular brushings help to whisk away pieces of debris, dust, dirt, and dead hair, and it releases lubricants from sebaceous glands, promoting and distributing the natural oils that bring out the shine and natural luster in a dog's coat.

How to Brush Your Stafford

Starting at your dog's head, brush the top of the head and around the ears, and go down the neck, chest, and front legs. Then, brush in one long stroke from the head toward the tail. Go down his sides and finish with his tummy and rear legs. Brush gently, and use care with slicker or wire brushes so as not to cause nicks, scratches, or even welts on his skin.

As you brush, pay particular attention to the condition of his coat. Your Stafford's coat is a mirror reflection of his health. Check to see:

- Is his coat healthy and glossy? Or is it dull, brittle, and lackluster?
- Is his skin dry and flaky?
- Does his skin have a bad smell or that unmistakable doggy odor?
- Do you see bare spots where hair is missing?

Any of these conditions could be a sign of inadequate grooming, internal illness, parasite infestation, or an inadequate diet. When in doubt, a veterinarian can diagnosis the problem and recommend suitable treatments.

After you're done brushing, finish the coat and add shine by rubbing it down with a chamois or soft towel and spraying or rubbing on a coat oil.

Bathing

How often your Stafford requires bathing depends on where you live, how much time he spends outside, and how dirty he gets. Like kids, some dogs tend to get dirtier than others. If he is your constant companion on walks, hikes, and trips to the barn, he may require bathing on a regular basis—say, every few weeks. If he spends a great deal of time indoors, he may require bathing once every 4 to 6 weeks. There is no cut-and-dried formula for how often your Stafford needs bathing. You be the judge.

In warmer climates, you may be able to bathe your dog outdoors with a garden hose, provided the water isn't too cold. Otherwise, a rubber mat on the bottom of a bathtub or shower stall will provide secure footing and prevent him from slipping.

How to Bathe Your Stafford

First, gather all the supplies you need—shampoo, conditioner, plenty of soft towels, and if available, a grooming apron. With lukewarm water, saturate your Stafford's entire body (a cotton ball placed in each ear will keep the water out), apply a dab of shampoo, and scrub away! Work the shampoo into the coat with your fingers or a rubber massage tool designed specifically for dogs. Scrub from head to toe, being careful to avoid the eye area. Don't forget his tummy, between his hind legs, under his arms, and behind his ears. Wipe around your Stafford's eyes with a damp cloth. Rinse his entire body thoroughly with lukewarm water, and rinse again and again. Residual shampoo can irritate the skin, as well as leave a dull film on the coat. If you are using a coat conditioner or skin remoisturizer, be sure to follow the directions carefully.

The Expert Knows

Doggy Bad Breath

Also known as *halitosis*, bad breath is generally indicative of something more serious, such as periodontal disease, diabetes, kidney disease, or gastrointestinal problems. Unless you have seen your precious pooch eat something particularly offensive, like spoiled garbage, squirrel guts, cat stools, or another dog's stools (or even his own stools)—yes, some dogs find this appetizing—it is best to have your dog examined by a veterinarian. If left untreated, some causes of bad breath can cause severe and even fatal complications.

After a roll in the dirt, a bath may be in order.

Towel dry your dog thoroughly, and don't forget to remove the cotton balls from his ears. Staffords dry pretty fast, so blow drying is usually not necessary. It is worth noting that wet dogs love to roll in whatever is handy, be it grass, dirt, mud, or gravel, so consider sequestering him in the house until he is dry. Otherwise, before you can say squeaky clean, he can quickly undo all your hard work!

Nail Care

Nail trimming is another grooming ritual and a necessary part of dog ownership. Few Staffords will wear down their nails naturally, and if your dog's nails make an unmistakable *click, click, click* sound as he walks across the floor, his nails are too long. Long nails can be broken, torn off, or snagged, and can scratch furniture, hardwood floors, and skin. They also can cause a Stafford a great deal of pain and discomfort, and they may become infected, which can require veterinary attention.

As with other aspects of grooming, introduce your Stafford to the practice of nail care at a young age. In the beginning, depending on the puppy's level of cooperation, you may want to simply touch the nail clipper to the puppy's nail and then offer plenty of praise. Then progress to clipping tiny bits of nail until the nail is trimmed.

In the beginning, you may need someone to help hold your dog, but once you get used to it, trimming your Stafford's nails is no more difficult than trimming your own. When in doubt, ask a veterinarian, groomer, or breeder to show you how to do it properly. Or have a professional trim them regularly, which can mean once a week or once a month—or somewhere in between—depending on your dog.

How to Trim Your Stafford's Nails

Dogs have a blood vessel that travels approximately three-quarters of the way through the nail. This vessel is called the "quick." As the nail grows, so too does the quick. Therefore, it is better to get in the habit of trimming tiny bits of nail on a regular basis rather than waiting for the nails to get too long. Clipping a dog's nails too short can cut the quick and cause bleeding. However, learning how to do it properly, using the correct equipment, and having a dog who accepts having his feet handled goes a long way toward reducing the odds of inadvertently nipping the quick.

A Stafford's black nails can make it difficult, if not impossible, to see the quick, so you'll have to feel for it. Examine the underside of the nail. You should see that the section closest to the paw is solid, while the tip—or hook—of the nail looks hollow, like a shell. You may be able to see or feel the slightest groove on the underside hook portion of the nail. To avoid nipping the quick, clip only the very tip of the nail and have some styptic powder nearby just in case.

If your Stafford has dewclaws, be sure not to overlook them in the trimming process. Dewclaws are the fifth digit on the inside of the front legs, usually 1 inch (2.5 cm) or so above the feet. If left unattended, they can curl around and grow into the soft tissue, not unlike an ingrown toenail on a human. Some breeders have the dewclaws removed, so your Stafford may or may not have them.

One of the easiest ways to trim the nails on the front feet is to have your dog sit. Lift and hold one foot about 6 inches (15.2 cm) or so off the

FAMILY-FRIENDLY TIP

Children and Grooming

Children make great grooming assistants—especially the younger ones, who are always willing to help out. Supervision is always necessary, and brushing is a great place to start because a Stafford's coat is short and easy to brush. You won't need to worry about tangles or pulling the hair too hard. Children should learn to brush gently in one direction, brushing the entire dog from head to tail.

For smaller kids, stand them in the tub and let them scrub away with plenty of shampoo. Teach them not to be too rough or boisterous, and tell your child to be calm so as not to excite the dog. Once the dog is thoroughly rinsed, she can help apply the conditioner and then help dry him.

Letting your child assist with grooming responsibilities teaches her about responsibility and compassion and helps her to build a mutually respectful and loving relationship with her dog.

ground, so that you can see what you are doing, then trim away. With young or inexperienced dogs, you may have to put the foot back down between nails. Much depends on how cooperative the dog is. With the rear nails, it is easier to have your dog stand; when he is doing so, lift the foot straight up off the ground about 4 or 6 inches (10.2 or 15.2 cm), and trim away. Some people find it easier to lift the rear foot and extend the leg backward, not unlike the position a horse's leg is in when you are working on his feet. Some people even have their dog lie on the floor. This works in a pinch, too. It is really a matter of preference, what is easiest, and what the dog will and will not tolerate.

Get your Stafford used to having his nails trimmed at an early age.

Ear Care

Along with regular dental care, you'll need to add ear cleanings to the list of routine grooming requirements. A Stafford's ear canal is warm, dark, and moist—an ideal site for bacterial or yeast infections, tumors, and parasites, such as ear mites. Unlike a human's ear canal, which is a basically a horizontal line from the side of the head inward to the eardrum, a dog's ear canal is somewhat L-shaped. The internal ear canal descends vertically before making roughly a 45-degree bend and then a jaunt to the eardrum—also known as the tympanic membrane. Debris loves to collect in the 45-degree bend of the ear canal.

A healthy ear should have a clean, healthy doggy smell—resembling the smell of beeswax, somewhat. A honey-colored wax in the ear is normal, but a crusty, dark substance may indicate problems, such as ear mites. An infected ear has an unmistakable foul odor. Ear infections are serious and should never be ignored or taken lightly. If your Stafford's ears have a discharge, smell bad, or if the canals look abnormal, red, or inflamed, or your dog is showing signs of discomfort, such as depression, irritability, scratching or rubbing his ears or head, shaking his head, or tilting it to one side—these can be signs of a problem. Seek veterinary attention right away. An ear infection left untreated can cause permanent damage to a dog's hearing.

How to Clean Your Stafford's Ears

Like your Stafford's other grooming regimes, ear care will take some getting used to. Again, start slowly and progress at a speed suitable to your dog's age and mental maturity. Once he is accustomed to having his ears touched, examine and clean his ears regularly—at least once a week. To remove dirt and debris, use an ear-cleaning product specifically designed for dogs. Place a few drops of cleaner into the dog's ear canal, and gently massage the base of the ear for about 20 seconds. This helps to soften and loosen the debris. Let your dog have a good head shake to eject the cleaning solution and debris from the ear canal. Next, apply some ear-cleaning solution onto a clean cotton or gauze pad. Gently wipe the inside ear leather (ear flap) and the part of the ear canal that you can see. Use a fresh cotton ball or gauze pad for the other ear. Remember the old adage, "Never stick anything smaller than your elbow in your ear"? The same concept applies to dogs. Never stick cotton applicator swabs or pointed objects into the ear canal, because this tends to pack the debris rather than remove it. More important, you risk injuring your dog's eardrum should you probe too deeply.

If you suspect problems, seek veterinary attention right away, and leave the probing to the experts.

Eye Care

A Stafford's eyes should be clear and bright, but sometimes debris accumulates around the rims.

How to Clean Your Stafford's Eyes

This debris can easily be cleaned by saturating a gauze pad with warm water. Starting at the inside corner of the eye, gently wipe out toward the outside corner of the eye. If you notice excessive tearing, redness, swelling, discoloration, or discharge, these may be signs of an infection. If you suspect something is wrong, do not hesitate to call your veterinarian.

Dental Care

Just as you take good care of your teeth, you must take good care of your Stafford's teeth. Like humans, dogs can experience painful toothaches, although some dogs may not physically exhibit signs of pain, or the signs may be subtle and overlooked by some owners.

Use an ear cleaning product and gently wipe out your Stafford's ears.

The importance of high-quality dental hygiene cannot be overstated. Plaque builds up quickly, resulting in tartar, bad breath, and gingivitis. Daily brushings at home help to remove plaque. If left unattended, the plaque hardens into tartar, which requires veterinary attention to remove and leads to periodontal disease, a progressive disease that can, in advanced cases, lead to decayed gums, infection, and liver, kidney, and heart damage. In the early stages, periodontal disease is generally reversible, provided your Stafford receives veterinary attention along with regular brushings at home. In advanced stages, the damage is considered irreversible because germs have been busy destroying your Stafford's teeth, gums, and bones.

How to Care for Your Stafford's Teeth

As with other aspects of grooming, it is much easier to begin introducing oral hygiene to a puppy, but it is never too late to begin. Again, start slowly and progress at a speed that is suitable for your dog's age and mental maturity. Put a small dab of doggy toothpaste on your index finger, and let your dog lick it. Praise him for being clever! Apply another dab on your finger, gently lift up his outer lips, and massage his gums. Ideally, it is best to massage in a circular motion, but in the beginning, be satisfied with simply getting your finger in your dog's mouth. Try to massage both top and bottom and the front gums, too. Watch out for those

SENIOR DOG TIP

Grooming the Older Dog

Senior Staffords require just as much grooming as their younger counterparts. Seniors love being fussed over, too, but their bodies are older and their joints are often stiff and sore, so they may not be able to tolerate long grooming sessions. Monitor your dog throughout the grooming process to be sure he is comfortable. At the first signs of fatigue, stop and give him a break. You may need to groom in short, multiple sessions throughout the day or week. Keep an eye out for irregularities, such as swelling, tender spots, lumps, bumps, rashes, and hot spots that could signal a problem.

In addition to regular brushings, your senior Stafford still needs his nails clipped. Nails that are too long are painful, and they make it difficult for older dogs to get around. Continue cleaning his ears and teeth and checking for signs of infection or tartar and gingivitis. And don't forget to reward him with a tasty chew toy for his patience and simply because he's adorable.

sharp baby teeth! Keep a positive attitude, and praise and reassure your Stafford throughout the process. Avoid wrestling with your dog or restraining him too tightly. This only hampers the process and makes him resistant to the necessary routine.

Dental hygiene is very important to your dog's health.

Once your dog is comfortable with this process, use a toothbrush, finger toothbrush, or a gauze pad wrapped around your finger. Let your dog lick some toothpaste off the toothbrush or gauze pad, and praise him for being clever! Lift the outer lips and expose the teeth. Most owners find it easiest to start with the canine teeth—the large ones in the front of the mouth. They are the easiest to reach, and you should be able to brush them with little interference or objection from your dog. Once your dog is accustomed to you brushing a few teeth, progress to a few more, and then a few more, until you have brushed all 42 teeth (or 28 teeth if you have a puppy).

Professional Teeth Cleaning

In addition to regular home dental care, your Stafford also requires annual dental exams, just as you do. A veterinarian will check for potential problems, such as tartar, gingivitis, periodontal disease, and fractured or abscessed teeth. Your veterinarian may recommend a professional dental cleaning, also known as prophylaxis or prophy. It's not unlike having your own teeth professionally cleaned. However,

your dog will be anesthetized to be sure that the veterinarian can do a thorough job of cleaning, inspecting, and repairing any damage. Fractured teeth may require reconstructive surgery, not unlike people receive, such as root canals and crowns.

Attire

Some Staffords, especially senior dogs, may need a winter coat in colder climates and canine booties to protect their feet from ice and snow. If you go this route, choose something dignified and functional that reflects his proud, noble heritage. Leave the sailor suits, bumblebee outfits, and polka dot dresses to the Chihuahuas and Poodles.

Grooming is a great way to spend quality time with your Staffordshire Bull Terrier. He will look and feel great, and you will have helped to enhance the human–canine bond.

Chapter 5

Feeling Good

An important part of canine ownership is being able to recognize when your dog is feeling a bit under the weather or facing a serious medical emergency. Just as you pay close attention to any symptoms that might indicate that your child has a cold or something more serious, such as the measles or chicken pox, you will need to know how to recognize when something is amok with your Stafford. Understanding what is normal will help you to recognize when something is amiss, and it will help to ensure that your adorable Stafford lives a happy and healthy life.

Finding a Veterinarian

Your Stafford is counting on you to take care of him, even when he's sick. To do this, you need a good veterinarian, and you want to find one right away, too—before you actually need one. Scanning the telephone book when your Stafford is sick or injured is never a good idea. Just as you invested a good deal of time finding the right Stafford, you must invest time and energy finding a suitable veterinarian with whom you feel comfortable asking questions, sharing concerns, and building a mutually trusting and respectful relationship.

Where to Look

Local telephone directories are a good starting point, as are animal-owning friends, relatives, neighbors, and coworkers. Ask your current veterinarian to refer you to some veterinarians if you are moving to a new town. Often the best referrals come from your Stafford breeder or local Stafford club. Most reputable breeders know several local veterinarians and specialists. Chances are good that the veterinarians recommended from these sources are familiar with the Stafford breed, and that's a good thing because you want a veterinarian who is not intimidated by these beautiful, highly intelligent, and strong dogs!

Choosing a Facility

Choosing the veterinary clinic that is best for you and your Stafford will depend on your personal preferences, such as a whether you prefer a male or female veterinarian, proximity to your home, office hours, cleanliness of the facility, and what services you require. Some clinics offer boarding kennels, grooming services, and retail shopping. Others offer weekend and after-hour emergency care.

Once you have narrowed down your selection, tour the clinic. When visiting clinics, be sure to speak with the staff, as well as the veterinarian. Are they knowledgeable, courteous, friendly, and receptive to your concerns? Are you comfortable talking with them and asking questions? Make a note of their office hours and after-hours emergency care policy. What

Puppies should have their first vet checkup right away.

types of services do they offer? Tour the entire facility, including examination rooms, the X-ray room, the operating and recovery rooms, and the boarding areas. Is the clinic neat and clean? Are there unpleasant odors? Is it organized? Noisy? Chaotic? Is there a fenced or grassy area where your Stafford can eliminate? Does the waiting area provide adequate room for separating large and small dogs, unruly dogs from nervous dogs, and rambunctious dogs from shy dogs?

The relationship between you and your veterinarian is important, so take your time and choose one with whom you will be comfortable for the next 10 to 15 years.

Your Stafford's First Veterinary Visit

Once you have found the perfect veterinarian for you and your Stafford, it is time to get your puppy an appointment. Ideally, you should get your new pooch to the veterinarian within 48 to 72 hours after acquiring him, to make sure that he has no

health problems. The veterinarian will check your Stafford's overall condition, including inspecting his skin, coat, eyes, ears, feet, lymph nodes, glands, teeth, and gums. She will take his temperature, listen to his heart and lungs, and feel his abdomen, muscles, and joints. She will be looking for anything out of the ordinary, as well as observing your dog's reaction to being handled. She should ask you about your puppy's eating and elimination habits as well.

Vaccinations have saved the lives of millions of dogs.

Jot down any relevant information beforehand so that you have it at your fingertips, such as the type of food your puppy eats, how much and how often he eats, how often he relieves himself, the color, shape, and size of his stools, and so forth. Bring a fresh stool sample with you so that your veterinarian can check it for parasites. Put the stool sample in a plastic bag or disposable container, and place the container inside a brown paper bag labeled with your name and your dog's name.

Make a list of any questions you want to ask, such as how much and what type of food your puppy should be eating, health concerns particular to this breed, vaccinations, neutering, and so forth. Take advantage of this time to establish a good verbal relationship with the veterinarian and her staff.

Vaccinations

Vaccinations are really important for your Stafford puppy because a number of infectious diseases can make him very sick. Vaccinations can help prevent these problems. The diseases that your veterinarian chooses to inoculate against will depend on your dog's lifestyle, where you live, and how much traveling you plan to do with your dog.

Vaccinations generally start being administered at 6 to 8 weeks of age, and continue every 3 weeks until the puppy is 16 weeks old. The breeder should have given you a copy of your puppy's vaccination schedule when you picked him up. Take this information with you to your puppy's first vet visit. After examining your Stafford and reviewing his medical records, your veterinarian will set up a continued vaccination schedule, including a rabies vaccination at the appropriate time. Veterinarians differ in their vaccination protocol, but most inoculate against these seven most common diseases:

1. **Coronavirus.** Spread through the stool of infected dogs, coronavirus is highly contagious. Rarely fatal to adult dogs but frequently fatal to puppies, symptoms include vomiting, loss of appetite, and diarrhea, which may lead to dehydration, further endangering puppies. Puppies less than 12 weeks of age are at the greatest risk.

2. **Distemper**. A primary cause of illness and death in unvaccinated puppies, distemper is a highly contagious viral disease similar to the virus that causes measles in humans. Spread through the air as well as through contact with an infected animal's stool or urine, distemper can spread rapidly through kennels or multiple-dog households. Symptoms include nasal and eye discharge, coughing, diarrhea, vomiting, and seizures. Distemper is an incurable and deadly disease that can affect dogs of all ages; however, puppies and senior dogs are most vulnerable.

3. **Hepatitis**. Spread primarily through direct contact with an infected dog's saliva, nasal discharge, and urine, infectious canine hepatitis affects the tonsils and larynx. As it enters the bloodstream, it can affect the eyes, liver, and kidneys. Initial symptoms include sore throat, cough, and occasionally pneumonia,

with advanced symptoms including increased thirst, vomiting, and diarrhea. Unvaccinated dogs of all ages are at risk. The mortality rate is high, but vaccination prevents the disease.

4. **Leptospirosis.** Leptospirosis is a highly contagious bacterial disease that is spread primarily through the urine of infected animals. Staffords who sniff a bush that has been urinated on or who drink contaminated water may pick up the bacteria, which penetrates mucous membranes or abraded skin. It spreads to the kidneys, liver, spleen, eyes, and nervous system and can cause fever, vomiting, muscle pain, abdominal pain, diarrhea, loss of appetite, weakness, and lethargy. Vaccinations usually prevent the disease, although leptospirosis does appear in different strains, and vaccination against one strain does not protect against all strains.

5. **Kennel Cough.** Also known as canine infectious *tracheobronchitis* or *bordetellosis*, kennel cough is highly contagious and normally characterized by a harsh, dry coughing or hacking, which may be followed by retching and gagging. The disease is airborne—meaning it is passed through the air—and can spread rapidly among dogs who live together. Dogs at shows, boarding kennels, grooming shops, veterinary clinics, and public or private dog parks are at an increased risk to exposure.

6. **Parvovirus**. A life-threatening virus,

Talk to your vet about a vaccination schedule for your Stafford.

parvo is spread through the stools of infected dogs. Symptoms include diarrhea (often dark or bloody), vomiting, and dehydration. The majority of puppies infected are under 6 months of age, with the most severe cases seen in puppies younger than 12 weeks of age. Immediate medical attention is necessary should your Stafford exhibit any of these signs, or if you suspect that your puppy has been around an infected puppy. The mortality rate is high, but vaccination helps prevent the disease.

7. **Rabies**. All warm-blooded animals— including humans—are at risk for contracting rabies. This highly infectious viral disease affects the brain, and mortality is high; the disease is almost always fatal once symptoms appear. Transmission is generally through the bite of a rabid animal. No cure is available. Vaccination is the best way to prevent infection, and properly vaccinated animals are at a relatively low risk of infection.

Parasites

Parasites. They sound grotesque, and to the average dog owner, they usually are. Unfortunately, it is highly likely that sometime within your Stafford's life, he will suffer from an external parasite (like fleas) or an internal parasite (like worms). Both types of parasites need treatment because, if left unchecked, they can cause debilitating and life-threatening problems.

External Parasites

Fleas and ticks can wreak havoc with your Stafford. Keeping one step ahead of these pesky creatures will help your canine companion stay healthy, happy, and comfortable.

Fleas

One bite from these pesky creatures can send your dog into a vicious cycle of scratching, biting, and digging at his skin. And where one flea exists, likely there are plenty more lurking on your precious Stafford—as well as in your carpet, furniture, and bedding. About ¹/₈ inch (0.3 cm) long and slightly smaller than a sesame seed, the *Ctenocephalides felis*, also known as the domestic cat flea, is the most common flea responsible for infesting dogs. Fleas are responsible for spreading tapeworms and causing serious allergic dermatitis. In serious infestations, fleas can cause anemia, especially in puppies.

The good news is that the advent of once-a-month topical treatments makes eradicating fleas a lot easier than it was 10 or 15 years ago. These treatments, which are applied to the dog's skin between the shoulder blades, are absorbed into his system, and the flea is killed when it bites the dog. Additionally, a number of shampoos, sprays, dips, and powders are available. These products have been around

for years, but many commercial and natural products may be toxic. They can irritate your Stafford's skin or cause health problems.

Although flea-control products are effective, they work best when used in conjunction with a rigorous flea-control problem. A flea collar alone will not provide your Stafford with a flea-free environment. To eradicate fleas, try these steps:

1. Clean everything your Stafford has come in contact with. Wash all dog beds and blankets, and mop up floors. Vacuum all carpets, rugs, and furniture. Immediately dispose of vacuum bags because eggs can hatch in them.

2. Remove dense vegetation near your home, dog yard, or kennel area—these spaces offer a damp microenvironment that fleas love and in which they thrive.

3. Treat your Stafford and any other household pets who can serve as hosts, such as other dogs, cats, and ferrets.

Ticks

Approximately 850 species of ticks exist—all of which burrow their heads into your Stafford's skin and engorge themselves with blood, expanding to many times their size.

Ticks are dangerous because they can secrete a paralysis-causing toxin and can spread serious diseases, including Lyme disease, Rocky Mountain spotted fever, and Texas fever. Ticks can also be infected with

Flea Fact

One flea can bite your Stafford up to 400 times a day.

Flea Allergy Dermatitis (FAD)

If your Stafford is sensitive to fleas, one bite from this tiny, nearly invisible pest can make his life (and yours!) miserable. Also known as *bite hypersensitivity*, flea allergy dermatitis tends to be most prevalent during the summer, when fleas are most rampant and annoying. Dogs with flea allergies may itch over their entire bodies, experience generalized hair loss, and develop red, inflamed skin and hot spots. Frequently restless and uncomfortable, they may spend a great deal of time scratching, digging, licking, and chewing at their skin. Treatments can be multi-faceted, including over-the-counter hypoallergenic or colloidal oatmeal-type shampoos to remove allergens and topical anti-itch creams to soothe the skin. Fatty acid supplements, such as omega-3 and omega-6 (found in flaxseed and fish oils) are helpful in reducing the amount and effects of the *histamine* your dog's body produces and which causes the inflammation and itch. In some cases, your veterinarian may prescribe something to help reduce itching.

and transmit more than one disease. In severe infestations, anemia and even death may occur.

Most ticks are picked up while walking or playing in wooded or grassy areas, overgrown fields, and near low, overhanging branches or shrubs. Ticks commonly embed themselves between the toes, in the ears, and around the neck but can be found elsewhere on your Stafford's body.

Controlling ticks is very similar to controlling fleas. Treat your house, yard, dog blankets, and your dog with products designed specifically for ticks. A number of over-the-counter products are available, but again, these products may be toxic. Read all labels and follow directions carefully.

If you do find a tick on your Stafford, remove it. This isn't terribly difficult—once you get past any queasiness about doing so. Use tweezers or a specially designed tick-removing tool to grab the tick as close as possible to where it enters your dog's skin. Pull slowly, firmly, and steadily in an outward direction. Clean the bite wound with a disinfectant and apply an antibiotic ointment.

If you simply cannot bring yourself to remove the tick, take your dog to the veterinarian. Ticks must be removed, and the sooner the better.

Internal Parasites

Endoparasites live inside your Stafford's body. Endo means *in*, hence their catchy name. The most common are heartworms, hookworms, roundworms, tapeworms, and whipworms. A number of deworming medications are available at pet stores and retail outlets. However, dewormers differ drastically in their safety and effectiveness in expelling worms from the body. So always have your veterinarian diagnose the specific type of internal parasite and prescribe the proper deworming medication.

Heartworms

Transmitted by mosquitoes, heartworms are potentially the most dangerous internal parasites because the larvae grow inside your healthy dog, migrating through his tissues into the bloodstream and eventually into his heart. The larvae grow into adult worms between 6 and 14 inches (15.2 and 35.6 cm) in length and can completely fill and obstruct the heart chambers and various large blood vessels leading from your dog's heart to his lungs.

A chronic cough is often the first symptom, followed by a decrease in appetite, loss of weight, listlessness, and fatigue after light exercise. Some dogs take on a pot-bellied appearance. Unfortunately, symptoms may not appear until the damage is extensive and the disease is well advanced.

Preventive medications are available and highly recommended. However, they must never be given to a dog who is already infected with adult worms. Therefore, always consult your veterinarian before starting any preventive treatment for heartworms.

Hookworms

About ½ inch (1.3 cm) long, hookworms can cause serious health problems for your puppy including diarrhea, vomiting, and life-threatening anemia. Symptoms may also include pale gums, weakness, and black, tarry stools.

Hookworms have teeth-like structures (hooks) that attach to the lining of your Stafford's intestine, feeding on his oxygen-carrying blood. Like other internal parasites, eggs are passed in the dog's feces, where they hatch into larvae. Dogs become infected when they ingest

Check your dog for fleas and ticks after he's been outside.

contaminated food or water, lick their contaminated feet, or ingest an infected host. Thus, the cycle of infestation continues. Puppies often become infected through their mother, but good sanitary practices will help prevent the spread of hookworms. This is why it's so important to pick up fecal material daily. Also, when walking in public places, do not allow your dog to come in contact with other dogs' feces.

Roundworms

Roundworms live in a dog's small intestine and can cause serious problems for dogs and huge headaches for owners. They absorb nutrients, interfere with digestion, and can damage the lining of your Stafford's intestine. In severe infestations, dogs may be thin and have a pot-bellied appearance. Other symptoms include dry, dull, and rough-looking coats. Some puppies have intestinal discomfort and may cry as a result.

Roundworms are resistant to environmental conditions and most common disinfectants. They can adhere to hair, skin, and paws, so good hygiene and strict sanitation practices are essential to minimize further contamination. Roundworms can live for months or even years once they get into the soil.

Tapeworms

Although not normally life threatening, tapeworms are a problem because they live in your Stafford's intestine, attach to the wall of the intestine,

First-Aid Kit

If you own a Staffordshire Bull Terrier, you should have a canine first-aid kit. Dogs have the uncanny ability to get into anything and everything and always at the most inopportune times. If your Stafford is sick or injured, always err on the side of caution and seek veterinary assistance.

Here are the basic ingredients for a doggy first-aid kit:

- activated charcoal
- alcohol or alcohol prep pads
- anti-diarrheal medicine
- eye wash or saline solution
- eye ointment
- gauze rolls and gauze pads
- gloves
- hydrogen peroxide
- important telephone numbers
- iodine
- lubricant
- muzzle
- pen and paper
- rehydrating solution
- scissors
- styptic pencil
- thermometer
- towels, blanket, or old sheet
- tweezers

and absorb nutrients. They grow by creating new segments, which makes getting rid of them especially difficult, because unless the head is successfully eliminated, they can grow a new body.

Tapeworms generally do not cause any symptoms, although diarrhea may be present. In severe infestations, dogs may exhibit abdominal discomfort, nervousness, or vomiting. Some dogs scoot their rear ends along the ground. Passed through the feces, tapeworms look like tiny grains of uncooked rice. Flea and lice control are essential, otherwise your Stafford will continue to reinfest himself.

Whipworms

Whipworms get their name from the whip-like shape of the adult worm. They live in the large intestine, where they feed on blood. Adult worms lay eggs that are passed in the feces. Mild infestations may not produce any obvious symptoms, but larger infestations can result in inflammation of the intestinal wall. Anemia is possible if hemorrhaging occurs. Other symptoms include diarrhea, mucus and blood in the stools, and weight loss. Whipworms can live in moist soil for years, so dogs who bury their bones or dig in the dirt or eat grass can pick up eggs. To help reduce or prevent contamination, fecal matter must be picked up daily, and kennel or dog run areas must be cleaned thoroughly.

Breed-Specific Illnesses

Staffords are a pretty healthy breed, with an average lifespan of around 12 years. However, like most breeds, Staffords are not immune to health problems.

Entropion and Ectropion

Entropion is a condition in which the lower eyelid, along with the eyelashes, rolls into the eye and rubs on the surface of the eyeball, causing irritation and possible damage and ulcerations of the cornea. One or both eyes may be involved, and in rare cases, the upper eyelid may also be affected. Symptoms include squinting, redness, and inflammation of the eye. Some dogs will scratch at their eye, possibly causing further damage. Examination of the eyelid will confirm the diagnosis. Surgery is the only treatment.

Ectropion, the opposite of

Bring your puppy to the vet if you suspect internal parasites.

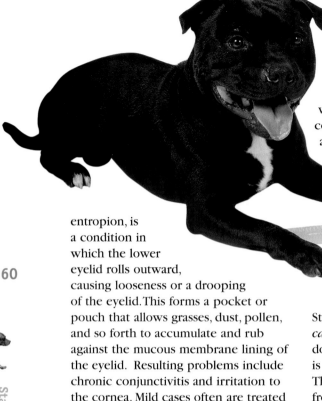

moving together.

Diagnosis is generally made through a combination of physical examinations and X-rays and by ruling out other problems with overlapping symptoms. Treatment varies and can include over-the-counter drugs, such as glucosamine and chondroitin, prescription medications, or even surgery.

Cataracts

Cataracts often resemble a cloudy film on the surface of a dog's eyes, and most people think of them as something only old dogs develop. But Staffords can also develop *juvenile cataracts* that show up in young dogs (which in the Stafford breed is generally up to 1 ½ years of age). These types of cataracts are inherited from a dog's parents. Cataracts may be very small and not affect a dog's vision, or they may cause partial or complete blindness. No medical treatment is available to prevent, reverse, or shrink cataracts. Surgery is the only known treatment, and new, improved techniques have increased the success of restoring vision to affected Staffords.

entropion, is a condition in which the lower eyelid rolls outward, causing looseness or a drooping of the eyelid. This forms a pocket or pouch that allows grasses, dust, pollen, and so forth to accumulate and rub against the mucous membrane lining of the eyelid. Resulting problems include chronic conjunctivitis and irritation to the cornea. Mild cases often are treated with eye drops or salves. Severe cases require surgery to remove excess tissue.

Hip Dysplasia

Hip dysplasia is a defect in the conformation of the hip joint that can cause weakness and lameness to a dog's rear quarters, resulting in arthritis and severe, debilitating pain. Symptoms can include a decrease in activity, stiffness in the rear legs after exercising or first thing in the morning upon rising, and walking or running with an altered gait or "bunny hop" gait, in which a dog runs with both hind legs

Mast Cell Tumors

Dogs have mast cells in their skin and other tissues, such as the intestines and respiratory tract, that participate in the war against parasites, and generally they cause no problems. These cells contain large amounts of histamine, heparin, and special enzymes that break down protein, which are released when triggered by a dog's immune system. Problems arise when a lot of mast cells form a mast cell tumor, which can be either malignant or benign.

How and why these mast cell tumors form is speculative, but there appears to be a hereditary factor, with most tumors developing in older dogs—usually around eight to nine years of age. Symptoms may include vomiting, ulcers, blood in the stool, and abnormal blood clotting, as well as a visible tumor, which can vary in its appearance. Diagnosis is usually made with a needle aspirate—meaning some tumor cells are collected with a needle and examined under a microscope. Tumors are graded from 1 to 4 through a tissue biopsy, with 4 being the most aggressive. Treatment and prognosis

varies depending on the dog, the tumor's grading, and location. Most require surgery to remove, with some requiring follow-up radiation and anti-cancer drugs.

General Illnesses

Common health problems are found in most breeds of dogs and may be present in some Staffords.

Allergies

Staffords, as well as dogs in general, can suffer from allergies—just as humans do. Some of the most common canine allergies include flea bite allergies (see sidebar on page 56), inhalant allergies (also known as atopic dermatitis), and food allergies.

Inhalant Allergies

Inhalant allergies are caused by a genetic predisposition and

61

Feeling Good

Staffordshire Bull Terriers are considered a healthy breed.

FAMILY-FRIENDLY TIP

Visiting the Vet With Your Child

An important part of canine ownership is scheduling (and keeping!) regular veterinary checkups for your Stafford. Bringing your child along will help her to learn about responsibility and the importance of taking good care of the family dog. However, veterinary clinics can be a bit scary for some young children—especially when they don't understand what's happening. To help make the experience less stressful for you, your child, and your Stafford, plan ahead and incorporate your child into the visit. For example, read basic canine health care books with her. Have her jot down a few questions to ask the veterinarian, such as how much her dog should weigh, how tall he should be, how often his nails need trimming, or how old the dog really is in human years. Also, jot down some information that your child can give to the veterinarian, such as how often you feed the dog, how much and what type of food, how often he goes to the bathroom, and so forth. Most clinics are accepting of well-behaved children, and veterinarians are usually willing to answer questions about their equipment, procedures, and so forth. After all, they were once inquisitive ten-year-olds, too! And who knows? Perhaps you'll spark your child's curiosity and she'll become a veterinarian someday.

hypersensitivity to environmental allergens, such as dust mites, mold spores, grass, and weed pollen. Exposure to these allergens—usually when pollen activity is high—triggers your dog's immune system, causing itchy and inflamed skin. Chewing, digging, scratching, and biting at the skin are primary symptoms, which can cause secondary skin infections. No definitive atopic dermatitis test exists, so veterinarians use a process of elimination. They first look at the dog's history and symptoms, then rule out other conditions, such as food allergies, flea infestation, parasites, and mange, which have similar symptoms. Although incurable, atopic dermatitis can often be controlled through immunotherapy and medications, such as antihistamines or steroids. Reducing your Stafford's exposure to triggering allergens, combined with the use of household filters, hypoallergenic shampoos, topical anti-itch creams, and omega-3 and -6 supplements can help when combined with veterinary treatment.

Food Allergies

Dogs also can be allergic to foods, including beef, chicken, dairy products, wheat, corn, and soy—the most common ingredients in dog food! Allergy symptoms are similar to those of atopic dermatitis—scratching, itching, chewing, hair loss, and red, inflamed, or irritated skin—and that can make diagnosing food allergies a bit tricky. Food trials—feeding a very specific diet for 12 weeks—are the most effective method of providing a definitive diagnosis. Treatment is pretty straightforward and requires owners to eliminate the offending food source from their dog's diet by feeding either a special commercially prepared diet or a homemade diet.

Cancer

Unfortunately, like humans, dogs also get cancer. That doesn't mean that your Stafford will be diagnosed with cancer, but being informed is your first line of defense.

Most of the time, experts do not know how dogs (or people) get cancer. There are many types of canine cancer, such as lymphoma, osteosarcoma, traditional cell carcinoma, and mammary and testicular cancer, to name a few, and many possible causes, including chemicals in the environment, sun exposure, assorted viruses and infections, and genetic factors.

In the simplest of terms, cancer

starts with one or a group of cells that have "gone wrong." Experts believe that these cells show up in a dog's body all the time, but his assortment of natural mechanisms destroys the cells before they run amok. When the cells escape the dog's natural mechanisms, cancer develops.

The treatment and prognosis of dogs with cancer varies depending on the type of cancer and its stage of development, with most cancer therapy involving surgery, radiation, chemotherapy, or a combination of

63

Feeling Good

Cancer: Know the Signs

There are certain cancer warning signs that every pet owner should commit to memory, including:

- asymmetrical swelling
- lumps and bumps
- wound that doesn't heal
- unexplained weight loss
- lameness that can't be attributed to an injury
- unexplained vomiting or diarrhea

Your veterinarian should check any of these signs without delay.

the three. Cutting-edge diagnostic and treatment equipment, such as CT scanners, nuclear accelerators, and top-notch medications for treatment and pain, are helping, but oftentimes the cost is prohibitive for many owners.

The good news is that for some dogs with cancer, the quality of life is very good and so too is the length of time to be shared. Remember, it is not about the number of days but the quality of days that you share with your pet.

Alternative Therapies

Does your Stafford need acupuncture? How about a skeletal or muscular adjustment? What about a good old-fashioned massage?

Alternative medicine has been around for thousands of years, and as the demand for alternative medicine for humans increases, so too does the demand for alternative veterinary medicine. Often called *complementary veterinary medicine*, alternative medicine broadly describes those methods and practices of medicine that are used in place of or in addition to conventional medical treatments. Traditional medicine is rooted in science, physics, chemistry, and biology, and its practices are backed by scientific data. Alternative medicine is empirical, meaning the evidence comes less from clinical trials and more from anecdotes and testimonials from veterinarians and dog owners.

Alternative medicine encompasses a broad range of treatments, including acupuncture, chiropractic care,

You might want to explore some alternative veterinary practices for your Stafford.

Staffordshire Bull Terriers

massage, herbal supplementation, and holistic medicine.

Countless stories have been told of dogs who have benefited from both traditional and alternative medicines. However, before investing in alternative medicine, consult your veterinarian for advice or a referral, or contact the American Veterinary Medical Association (AVMA), which has established veterinary guidelines for many of these practices.

This chapter has outlined a few of the problems you might encounter with your Stafford. That's not to say that your dog will develop any of these conditions, and hopefully he will live a long, healthy, and happy life. However, the more informed you are about canine health issues, the more likely you are to recognize when something is amiss.

SENIOR DOG TIP

Keeping Your Senior Stafford Comfortable

Your Staffordshire Bull Terrier will be a senior citizen at approximately 8 years of age.

Most veterinarians recommend yearly checkups, with some preferring bi-annual checkups—especially for dogs 7 years of age and older.

Your senior dog may show signs of slowing down, as well as of age-related illnesses including arthritis, obesity, deafness, and cataracts. His bladder control may weaken, leading to accidents in the house.

Make your Stafford's senior years comfortable by continuing to feed him a healthy diet. Glucosamine and chondroitin supplements may help to ease his potpourri of aches and pains, as will a comfortable bed and a good canine massage. Be sure to give him plenty of physical and mental exercise daily, and continue to groom him regularly. Lots of love and attention will carry him through the day. And don't forget to remind him that he's still your little tough guy—even in his senior years.

65

Feeling Good

Chapter 6

Being Good

Bringing your new puppy home is very exciting! His cuddly good looks and puppy antics make him irresistible—but don't let his cute appearance deceive you. At an early age, he quickly can learn to manipulate you, so you must start to instill positive behaviors, basic obedience commands, and household rules right away.

As your puppy grows bigger and bolder and ventures through canine adolescence, your training plans and good intentions may fall by the wayside when he chooses to ignore your commands, bolts out doors, jumps on people, or swipes food off the supper table. The good news is that most of these problems are predictable. Armed with a good game plan and a bit of knowledge, many of these problems are entirely preventable. At the very least, you can keep them from escalating into major stumbling blocks, thereby keeping your puppy from growing into an unruly hooligan.

Why the Training Fuss?

A well-behaved Stafford is a joy to live with because he is fun to have around. As a result, he is more likely to be included in day-to-day activities and family outings. A well-trained Stafford can be trusted not to jump on visitors, chew your shoes, or pee from one end of the house to the other. No doubt his life is more enjoyable, too, because a trained Stafford is more likely to included in family activities rather than relegated to the social isolation of the backyard or surrendered to the animal shelter.

Years ago, the accepted methodology of dog training was that a puppy had to be at least six months old before you began teaching basic obedience skills. That concept has since been debunked, and modern-day breeders, trainers, and animal behaviorists now recognize the important benefits of early training—as early as 8 weeks of age. Additionally, trainers from the past often employed

Staffords have a natural love of children, but they still need proper socialization.

How to Find a Trainer

Puppy classes are a lot of fun, and you should consider enrolling your Stafford in one. Puppy classes help your puppy expand on the social skills he learned from interacting with his mother and littermates. Puppy classes should not be a free-for-all however, where puppies play on their own while their owners socialize on the sidelines. A well-structured puppy class begins instilling basic obedience skills and fun puppy games.

Here are some things you should do and look for when choosing a trainer for your Stafford:

- Ask your veterinarian, breeder, dog groomer, or dog-owning friends for referrals.
- Attend the classes of several trainers to observe their personalities, training techniques, and facilities. Training should be fun and humane. Hitting, kicking, electronic collars, or any other training device that causes harm should never be used.
- Look for trainers who focus on rewarding what your Stafford does right rather than punishing what he does wrong.
- Classes should be structured and run smoothly, yet still emphasize fun.
- The facility should provide a safe learning environment for you and your puppy, with plenty of lighting, matted floors, and eight to ten puppies per class.
- Small puppies should be separated from large puppies; young puppies from junior dogs; and the rambunctious from the shy.

the standard "pop and jerk" type training that involved a choke chain, force, and total domination of the dog. While the method generally produced desired results, it often came at a hefty price that included stifling a dog's personality, as well as his willingness and desire to please. Many of those methods produced dogs who obeyed commands out of fear rather than a desire to please their owners.

Today's top trainers recognize the importance of allowing dogs and handlers to be themselves, rather than imposing the same training method regardless of temperament. While you can still find trainers who adhere to the ideology of force and domination as a means of training, most trainers today employ gentler training methods that include praise, positive motivation, and positive reinforcement.

The concept behind positive motivation/reinforcement is that a favorable consequence to a behavior encourages repetition of that behavior.

A dog learns to repeat a behavior, such as *sit, down,* or *come,* to receive a reward, be it a tasty tidbit of food, a toy, or a giant kiss on the nose—or a combination of all three!

Socialization

Between 8 and 16 weeks of age is a critical socialization period for your Stafford. What happens during this timeframe has a significant impact on his future behavior as an adult. Squandering your opportunities during this time means that you run the risk of having your puppy develop bad habits and associations that are difficult, if not impossible, to correct later in life.

Between 8 and 12 Weeks of Age

When you bring your new puppy home, usually between 8 and 10 weeks of age, plan to spend a lot of time with him maximizing his future, fostering his zany personality, instilling desired behaviors, and squelching undesirable ones. For the first few days, your puppy will be adjusting to you, his new home, and life without his doggy mom and littermates. In the weeks to come, he will feel safe sticking close to you and following you everywhere. This is the perfect time to begin exposing him to all the sights and sounds he is likely to encounter as an adult dog, such as other animals, people in floppy hats, the clapping of hands, and the clatter of dog bowls. It's also the perfect time to accustom him to handling and grooming. Check his teeth, count his toes, rub his tummy, and kiss his nose. Brush his coat, clip his nails, inspect his ears, and rub your hands over his entire body. This helps you to bond with your puppy and teaches him to trust your hands. He must learn to have his body touched and examined without throwing a tantrum.

Between 12 and 16 Weeks of Age

Between 12 and 16 weeks, your puppy will be bigger, bolder and more confident. He won't need you quite as much as he used to, and he may choose to ignore your commands. He is checking to see if the

With proper socialization and training, your Stafford can get along with many types of animals.

household rules will be enforced. This is a critical juncture in the human–canine relationship. You mustn't become complacent. Make sure that everyone in the household is enforcing household rules consistently.

If you do nothing else for your puppy, you owe it to him to make the time to properly and adequately socialize him during this critical life stage. Yes, it's time consuming, but it is a necessary and obligatory investment when you choose to own a Staffordshire Bull Terrier. His future well-being depends on how much you do—or fail to do—during this critical period.

Crate Training

A crate placed in a quiet corner of your kitchen or family room will replicate a dog's natural instinct to seek a safe and secure environment. When properly introduced, a crate becomes a safe zone for your Stafford—a quiet place all his own in which to sleep, eat, and retreat from the demands of being a puppy, not to mention the prodding fingers of noisy, rambunctious toddlers.

A crate is a safe and efficient way to housetrain a young puppy or adult dog. It's also ideal for keeping your Stafford safe while traveling. A crated dog will not distract you from your driving responsibilities, teethe on your armrests, ransack the grocery bags, snatch french fries from the cashier at the drive-up window, or eat your cell phone. Many motels and hotels, as well as friends and family, are more receptive to dogs provided they are crate trained. As your Stafford grows and matures, the crate will continue to be his den and safe place for eating, sleeping, and retreating from the often chaotic and noisy world of humans.

How to Crate Train Your Stafford

Most puppies quickly learn to love their crate when it is associated with good things, such as feeding, yummy treats, security, and sleep. To maximize the training process, make the crate attractive to your puppy by placing a cozy crate pad, old blanket, or rug and a few of his favorite indestructible chew toys inside the crate. Remember, puppies love to chew, so you might want to hold off on that expensive crate pad for the time being, and be sure to choose toys that don't present a choking hazard. Leave the crate door open and allow your puppy to explore in and around the crate. When he goes inside the crate, praise him. Reward him with a tasty tidbit while he is in the crate, but don't close or latch the door just yet.

For the reluctant puppy, encourage him by letting him see you toss a tasty tidbit of food inside the crate, preferably toward the back. Incorporate your kids in the training process by allowing them to be the designated cookie tosser. When your puppy goes inside the crate to retrieve the food, praise him. You can also begin introducing a cue phrase, such as "Go to your kennel" or "Kennel up" as he goes inside the crate. Leave the door closed for longer and longer periods of time.

Feed your puppy inside his crate, too. He may charge right in and wait for his food. If so, praise him for being brave. For a reluctant puppy, place his food bowl inside the crate, close to the opening. With each feeding, move the food closer to the back of the crate until he is going inside to eat, but leave the door open. Be patient, progress in small steps, and remember to reward positive behavior. If your puppy whines or cries, avoid reinforcing the behavior by letting him out of the crate or coddling him. Wait for him to be quiet

Crate training makes housetraining your puppy much easier.

Doing It on Cue

By going outside with your puppy, you begin to instill a verbal cue for the command to eliminate, such as "Go pee" or "Go potty." These verbal cues should be given each time your puppy is in the *process* of urinating or defecating. Otherwise, you will teach him the wrong association. The words should be said in a calm but encouraging tone of voice. If your voice is too excitable, your puppy will likely forget what he is doing and run to see what you are so excited about.

for a few seconds before opening the door.

As your puppy becomes more comfortable with the crate, gradually increase the time he spends there. Never confine him for longer than 1 or 2 hours at a time—except at night when he is sleeping.

Housetraining

Crate training and housetraining go hand in hand, which makes the latter process relatively simple. Most den animals have an instinctive desire to keep their dens clean, so they avoid eliminating there. A crate serves as your puppy's den.

How to Housetrain Your Stafford

Young puppies have little or no bladder control until around 5 months of age. They also mature at different rates, so your puppy's control may develop earlier or later. As he matures, he will gradually learn to hold his bladder for longer periods of time. Puppies also are

most active during the day—running, jumping, training, playing, exploring, and just being a puppy. Because of their limited bladder size and lack of control, they are going to need to relieve themselves many, many times throughout the day. During the night, however, puppies are usually exhausted from their busy day. They are more relaxed at this time, so most can sleep between 5 and 8 hours without having to potty. If your puppy wakes you up in the middle of the night or in the early morning because he needs to go, it is always better to get up with him. The fewer accidents he has in his crate, the less stressful the process will be. Although it may seem like forever, it will not be long before he can hold on all night.

For the first several months—until your puppy begins to develop some reliable bladder control—you must take him outdoors frequently. When you are 100 percent committed to a regular schedule, your puppy will quickly learn that relieving himself occurs on schedule.

Paper training is an alternative to crate training.

As a general guideline—to increase your chances of success while minimizing accidents—take your puppy outdoors at the following times:

- First thing in the morning when he wakes up and at least once every hour throughout the day.
- About 15 minutes after drinking water.
- About 30 minutes after eating.
- Immediately after waking from a nap.
- When you arrive home from work.
- Any time you take him out of his crate.
- Last thing at night.

This guideline is for young puppies, and you may need to tweak or adjust this schedule to fit your puppy's individual needs. No one said raising a puppy was all fun and no work! Housetraining a puppy is a time-consuming endeavor, but time invested at this stage will make your life easier in the long run.

Housetraining Accidents

Few owners escape puppy rearing without an accident or two. However, it is in your and your Stafford's best interest to keep accidents to a minimum. Prevention is key. Never put your puppy in a position where he can make a mistake. Watch him like a hawk at all times, and never give him free run of the house. During those times when you can't keep him in your sights, such as when you are showering, getting dressed, or making dinner, confine him in his crate or exercise pen with a tasty chew toy, or tether his leash to your waist or a chair. If you see him start to circle, sniff around, or walk in circles, immediately take him outside to his bathroom spot. Watch him to make sure that he empties his bladder or bowels. It may take a few minutes, so be patient. While your puppy is in the process of relieving himself, calmly praise him with "Good puppy!" or "Good potty!"

If you take your puppy outdoors and he does not relieve himself, it is important that you put him back in his crate for 5 or 10 minutes, then repeat the aforementioned steps. (If you are not using a crate to housetrain, keep your puppy where you can watch him like a hawk for those 5 or 10 minutes.) Do this as many times as necessary until you see your puppy relieve himself outdoors. Never assume your puppy has done his business.

Why go to all this trouble? This helps establish the habit of using a certain area of your yard, and it helps to keep your puppy on track, thereby preventing him from getting too distracted with the potpourri of outdoor sights, smells, and sounds. Puppies are naturally curious and easily distracted, but if yours gets too distracted and forgets to go—guess where he's going to go when you bring him back indoors and he's no longer distracted? Also, young puppies, generally under the age of 3 months, find comfort and security in being close to you. If you leave while your puppy is searching for a spot to potty, he will likely run after you and forget

FAMILY-FRIENDLY TIP

How to Involve Your Child in Training

Children, especially the young ones, love to be included in any activity that involves a dog, be it brushing, feeding, or training. Including your children in the training process helps to teach them responsibility and compassion, and they can have a great deal of fun in the process.

Here are some ways to get your child involved:

- Read training books and watch training DVDs together.

- Allow your child to attend puppy kindergarten and obedience training classes with you and your dog. Some classes allow children 8 years and older to help with the training.

- Let your child be responsible for keeping track of the training equipment—leash, toys, treats, and so forth.

- Under your supervision, allow your child to play chase recall and retrieve games with your dog.

about the task at hand. In addition, by going outside with your puppy, you can praise him for doing what you want, which is going to the bathroom outdoors. This helps your puppy to understand exactly what you want and maximizes the learning process.

If your puppy has an accident in the house, simply clean up the mess and resolve to be more diligent. Never scold or hit your puppy, and never, ever rub his nose in the mess. Punishing, yelling, or otherwise berating your puppy will only confuse him and prolong the housetraining process.

Basic Obedience

The object of teaching basic obedience skills is to provide your Stafford with a set of commands he understands, making your life and his more enjoyable. Trying to physically restrain a 30-pound (13.6-kg) Stafford who wants to zig when you want to zag is enough to make you wish you had bought a cat.

Puppies and adult dogs learn through repetition and consistency. Therefore, to provide your puppy with a basic foundation of obedience skills and manners, you must be consistent with your expectations. Your Stafford must trust you. He should not worry about how you are going to react from day to day. For example, it is unfair to allow an 8-week-old puppy to jump on you today but scold him for doing so tomorrow, when his feet are muddy. It is equally unfair to feed your dog at the table every night, then act mortified and correct him when he begs your in-laws for tidbits of steak and potatoes. Think ahead. Decide which behaviors you will or will not accept and which behaviors you can or cannot live with for the next 12 to 14 years.

Equally important, puppies have limited attentions spans and are easily distracted by kids playing, birds singing, horses whinnying, and so forth. Expecting a young puppy to ignore distractions and focus entirely on you is unreasonable. Always set your puppy up to succeed by starting his training in a familiar environment that has a limited amount of distractions. Your living room or yard is ideal.

Reward your puppy when he recognizes his name.

Name Recognition

Teaching your puppy his name is relatively easy. Start with a pocket full of tasty treats. Stand close to your puppy, and say his name in a fun, happy voice. When he looks at you, reward him with verbal praise and a tasty tidbit. Practice this several times a day, and it won't be long before he knows his name.

Sit

Think of the many situations in which your Stafford will need to know how to sit—at the vet's office, waiting to be fed, or sitting and waiting while you open any door. He will need to sit when you put his collar on or take it off, when you want to check his coat for stickers or burrs, and when you want to brush him or trim his nails.

Teaching the *sit* command is relatively simple, and the guidelines are the same whether you are teaching a young puppy or an adult dog.

1. Start by showing your puppy a tidbit of food. Hold it close to and slightly above his nose.

2. Slowly move the treat in a slightly upward and backward direction toward his tail, keeping the treat directly above his nose. If your puppy's front feet come off the ground, the treat is too high. If he walks backward, the treat is too far back or too low.

3. When done correctly, your puppy's hips will automatically touch the ground. Give the *sit* command as your puppy's rear end hits the

The Expert Knows

Training Treats

When training your Stafford, use extremely tasty tidbits, such as pieces of hot dog, cheese, leftover tidbits of steak or chicken, liver, or peanut butter. Increase the incentive, and your puppy's motivation increases tenfold. Also, use tasty tidbits that are small enough for your puppy to swallow quickly. You don't want him standing around for 30 seconds chomping on a humongous biscuit. Plus, tiny tidbits won't add up to many calories, which will help keep off those extra pounds (kg).

ground. Praise with "Good sit!" and reward him with the treat.

4. Release your puppy with a release word, such as "Okay," play with him for a few seconds, and repeat the exercise three or four times in succession, three or four times a day.

Down

Down is an equally important and useful command. Your dog may need to lie down when the vet examines him, while you brush or scratch his tummy, or when you want to massage his sore muscles.

1. Begin by kneeling on the floor, so

Being Good

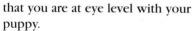
To teach sit, *slowly raise the treat over your dog's head.*

that you are at eye level with your puppy.

2. With him standing in front of you, hold a tasty tidbit of food in one hand. While your puppy is sniffing the tidbit, move it toward the floor between his front paws.

3. When done correctly, your puppy will plant his front feet and fold his body into the *down* position as he follows the food to the ground.

4. When your puppy is in the *down* position, reward with the treat and calmly praise him with a "Good down."

5. Release your puppy with a release word, such as "Okay," and repeat the exercise three or four times in succession, three or four times a day.

Stay

The goal of this command is to teach your dog to stay in a specific position, such as in a *sit* or *down*, until you say it is okay to move. It is useful in a variety of situations, such as when you want to open the door without your dog bolting through it.

Most Staffords are not emotionally mature enough to cope with this exercise until they are 5 or 6 months old. If this is the case with your puppy, do not force the issue. Simply wait until he is older and mentally mature enough to understand the exercise. To teach *sit-stay:*

1. Start with your puppy on a loose leash, sitting beside you.

2. Tell your puppy "Sit" and "Stay."

3. Watch your dog closely for the slightest movement that may indicate he is about to stand up or lie down. Be proactive in your training by reminding your dog to stay before he moves. If you see any movement, repeat your *stay*

command firmly but not harshly.

4. Once he has remained in position for a few seconds, praise him calmly and warmly with "Good stay" and a treat. Include calm, physical praise, such as gentle stroking—but not so enthusiastically that he gets excited and forgets the task at hand.

5. Release him with the word "Okay" or "Free." (If you release your dog first and then reward him, you will teach him the wrong association. He will think that he is being rewarded for moving. This can teach a puppy to anticipate the reward, thereby encouraging him to break the *stay* command.)

Do not be in a hurry to move away from your dog or have him hold the position for longer periods. Progress in 5-second increments until your dog can remain sitting beside you for 2 or 3 minutes without moving. Gradually begin increasing the distance between you and your dog

To teach the *down-stay*, begin with your dog in the *down* position, and tell him to stay. Then follow the remaining instructions for the *sit-stay*. To avoid confusing your Stafford, always teach the *down-stay* and *sit-stay* on different days.

Come

The goal of this command is to teach your puppy to come to you reliably, willingly, and immediately—without hesitation—upon hearing the command. He must come reliably even when in a wide range of situations, such as at the park, in an emergency, anytime he gets loose, and even when he's playing with his canine buddies.

In the beginning, teach this behavior with fun games and tasty rewards. Ideally, though, as your puppy grows into an adult dog, you want him to come to you because he wants to be with you—not just because you have a treat.

Use an informal game like "find me!" to begin teaching the *come* in a positive, fun, and exciting manner. This game capitalizes on a dog's natural chase instinct and is excellent for instilling the *come* command in young puppies.

1. Start with a pocket full of tasty tidbits.

Make sure that you teach come *in a safely enclosed spot.*

SENIOR DOG TIP

Helping Older Dogs

Older dogs in new homes with new owners can forget their manners and previous obedience training. They aren't naughty or dumb or purposely peeing on the carpet to annoy you. More than likely, they are nervous or disoriented in their new surroundings. They may not have been housetrained or obedience trained. It's difficult to know why some older dogs do what they do—especially when you acquire them later in their lives.

To help your older Stafford adjust to life in his new home, try these tips:

- Establish a routine and stick to it. Dogs are creatures of habit, and they do best when they have order in their lives.
- Always assume that your older dog is neither housetrained nor obedience trained. Begin all of his training as if he were a little puppy.
- Feed him a good-quality, well-balanced dog food, which he may or may not be accustomed to.
- Stay close to your older dog. Let him know that you are nearby. This will provide him with some comfort and security.
- Supervise your older dog at all times. Never allow him to go on unsupervised excursions where he can get himself into trouble.
- Take him for walks in the park and rides in the car. Play interactive games, and teach him obedience commands. This helps with the bonding process and builds his confidence.
- Love him unconditionally.

2. Rev up your puppy (or adult dog) by showing him a yummy treat, and then toss the treat down the hallway or across the living room.

3. As your puppy runs for the treat, run in the opposite direction and hide behind a chair or door as you say his name enthusiastically.

4. When your puppy finds you, make a big fuss: Get on the floor, roll around, and lavish him with a potpourri of kisses and praise.

5. Repeat the game several times throughout the day, but not so many times that your puppy becomes bored.

You can also play this game outdoors, but be sure to play in a fenced area to protect your dog from harm or prevent him from running away. When you are outside in your garden or yard with your dog and he stops to sniff the grass or explore a bug, duck behind a tree or bush, clap your hands, and say his name in an exciting tone of voice. When he finds you, reward with verbal praise and a tasty tidbit. It is not necessary for your dog to sit before he gets the treat. If you insist that your puppy sit before getting his treat, you will not be rewarding the most important part of the exercise, which is coming to you.

A puppy who views *come* as a fun game is more likely to develop a reliable response to the command. If this behavior continues throughout his puppyhood, and you remain excited and enthusiastic each and every time he comes to you, you will have a strong and positive response to the command as he matures into an adult dog.

Walk on Leash

If your puppy has been dragging his leash everywhere he goes—both indoors and outdoors—he's probably accustomed to it, so teaching him to walk on leash isn't terribly difficult. It is always easier to teach your puppy to walk on leash by starting on the left side and sticking with it until he understands the exercise. Once he has mastered walking nicely on leash, you can allow him to walk on either side or out in front of you.

Walking on leash should always

be something fun that you and your puppy do together. His leash and collar should never be associated with a barrage of nagging and corrections. To begin:

1. Always teach this exercise on a buckle collar, never a choke chain.

2. Attach a leash (or thin long line) to his collar and allow him to drag it around.

3. When your puppy is happily dragging the leash, pick it up and start walking forward, encouraging him to walk close to your left side by talking sweetly to him and luring him with a tasty tidbit from your left hand.

4. When you have walked a few steps with your puppy on your left side, reward him with the tidbit of food. Remember to verbally praise and offer the food reward when he is close beside your left leg. This encourages him to remain in position.

Once your puppy is comfortable walking beside you, you can begin teaching a more formal heel.

The training tips in this chapter only touch the surface of what is possible with your Stafford. Once he is socialized, crate trained, housetrained, and knows the basic commands, there is no end to the fun that you can have together.

Chapter 7

In the
Doghouse

In a perfect world, your Staffordshire Bull Terrier
would never get into trouble. In the real world,
however, it is unrealistic to expect your dog (or
any dog!) to go through his entire life without
getting into some sort of mischief or developing
an annoying habit or two. Keep in mind that some
of the "problems"—such as digging, barking,
and chewing—are natural behaviors for your dog.
However, if left unchecked, these natural behaviors
often turn into annoying habits.

As guardian of your puppy, it is your job to teach him which behaviors are acceptable and which are not. But how do you keep your Stafford out of the doghouse? First, it's important to realize that annoying or offensive behaviors do not appear suddenly. They are learned. Your dog will not shred your couch or pee indoors indiscriminately just to annoy you. His brain is not hardwired to be vindictive. If he's committing heinous crimes against your personal property, chances are he's not being properly supervised.

Equally important, puppies do not magically outgrow problems. A puppy who digs holes in your garden will not suddenly stop digging, regardless of how much you hope that he does. If you do not want him jumping on you, ransacking the trash, or digging to China under your prize rose bushes, you must modify his environment so that he is not put in a position where he can get himself into trouble.

If your Stafford has already developed some bad habits and is well on his way to wearing out his welcome, it's not too late to get him out of the doghouse and back into your good graces. Let's look at some common problem behaviors, including barking, chewing, digging, jumping up, and running off or not coming when called.

Barking (Excessive)

Overall, the Stafford is not a noisy dog, and excessive or chronic barking is generally not a problem. However, some dogs like to vocalize, and they need to be taught to stop barking. Dogs naturally bark or otherwise vocalize, and they do so for various reasons and at various times, including when they get excited, when they are playing with other dogs, when the doorbell rings, and to greet you when you arrive home.

Teaching your Stafford appropriate behaviors will keep him out of the doghouse.

Solution

If you can quiet your Stafford with a single command (or two!), you probably don't have much to worry about. Problems arise when your dog is too hyped up to stop barking, and that's why curtailing this problem early on is a necessity. This includes never encouraging your Stafford to bark. For example, when the doorbell rings, avoid asking your dog "Who's there?" or "Let's go see!" This can excite your Stafford and encourage him to bark. It may seem like a fun game when he is 10 or 12 weeks old, but it is a difficult and annoying behavior to stop once it becomes ingrained.

Avoid soothing or coddling your Stafford when he is barking. This, too, will inadvertently encourage the unwanted behavior. If your dog is barking, and you are telling him "It's okay, honey. Mommy loves you," he will think that he is being rewarded for barking. He figures "When I bark, my mom tells me it's okay. So I should keep barking."

Remember to always praise the behavior you want, which is not barking. For example, the moment that your dog stops barking, praise him with "Good quiet!" or "Good boy! That's what mommy wants!" Fortunately, most barking problems can be avoided if you plan ahead, understand why your dog is barking, and have a clear picture of the behaviors that you will and will not accept.

The best prevention against future barking problems is smart dog management:

FAMILY-FRIENDLY TIP

What Children Should Learn

Children who are raised with dogs must understand that not all dogs are as lovable and well behaved as their own Stafford. To keep your children safe, teach them these things:

1. Ask permission before petting a strange dog.

2. Offer their hand with their palm facing up (like feeding sugar cubes to a horse). Some dogs hate to be patted on the head and will shy away or possibly nip

3. Never go into a house or yard where a dog is present unless the owners are in attendance.

4. Stay away from chained, fenced, or stray dogs.

5. Always get help from an adult when dealing with an injured dog, because they are more likely to bite as a reflex to the pain.

6. Never stare directly at a dog. The dog may perceive this as a challenge.

- Never allow your puppy or adult Stafford to be put in a situation in which he is allowed to develop bad habits. Leaving him in the backyard

A dog left unsupervised in the backyard all day may develop a barking problem.

unsupervised all day may inspire him to bark at constant stimuli, including other dogs barking, a cat on a fence, a bird overhead, leaves falling, neighbors coming and going, and life in general.

- Barking at environmental stimuli is often self-rewarding for the dog. A dog barks at the mail carrier, and when the mail carrier leaves, the dog thinks, "Look how clever I am! My barking made that person leave!"

- A Stafford housed indoors can also develop barking habits. If he sits on the furniture and stares out the living room window, he may be encouraged to bark at stimuli, such as neighbors, other dogs going for a walk, or kids on bicycles.

- If your dog barks while in the excitement of play, halt the game immediately. When he stops barking, praise him with a "Good quiet!" or "Good boy!" Once you have regained control of the situation, begin playing again.

Chewing

It is hard to imagine your adorable 10-week-old Stafford puppy as a one-dog demolition team. However, do not let his cute looks deceive you. Stafford puppies, like most puppies, can be incredibly aggressive chewers and wreak havoc in your household. They will gleefully shred pillows, magazines, rugs, carpet, plants, and anything else they can get their teeth on—and that's in the 15 minutes it takes you to drive to the post office and back!

Puppies love to chew. It's a fact of life. They also *need* to chew, especially when they are teething. Teething varies from puppy to puppy, with most puppies undergoing some form of continuous teething until they are about 6 to 9 months of age. As their baby teeth fall out and their adult teeth erupt, it stimulates an uncontrollable urge to chew as a means of relieving some of the discomfort and as a way to facilitate the removal of their baby teeth.

Solution

Knowing this ahead of time, take steps to manage your puppy's environment so that he does not get himself into trouble. Puppy-proof inside and outside your home. Pick up anything and everything your Stafford is likely to seek out and destroy, such as shoes, purses, books, magazines, electrical cords, and so forth. If you must leave—even for 2 minutes—take your Stafford with you or confine him in a crate, exercise pen, or kennel. Do not put your puppy in a position where he can develop bad habits. This point cannot be emphasized enough. You must closely supervise your puppy anytime he is not confined. If you leave your Stafford unattended or unconfined while you run to the mailbox or take a quick shower, don't be surprised when you find the heel missing off your favorite pair of shoes.

A variety of chew toys are available in all sizes and shapes to entertain your Stafford for an hour or two. Chew toys will satisfy your puppy's need to gnaw on something while diverting him from chewing on inappropriate items. Although some chew toys are better than others, there is no scientific formula for finding the right chew toy. It's really a matter of trial and error. Avoid toys or bones that are too hard and that may crack your dog's teeth, or those that are too small or break apart and present choking hazards.

It is impossible to arbitrarily put an age on when a puppy is reliably trained. Some puppies have a stronger desire to chew than others. A general guideline is that most puppies pass the chewing stage at about 1 year of age.

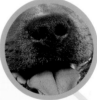

The Expert Knows

Call in the Professionals

Despite your best efforts to raise a well-behaved Staffordshire Bull Terrier, undoubtedly, times will arise when things go terribly wrong, and you may need to call in an expert. Some problems, such as aggression and separation anxiety, are difficult and complicated areas of canine behavior that require expert guidance. If you feel that you and your dog need expert advice, don't hesitate to seek it. You will both be much happier in the long run!

Teething causes puppies to have an uncontrollable urge to chew. (left) Your dog may be digging out of frustration or boredom. (bottom right)

Much depends on how conscientious and committed you are to managing your puppy's environment, instilling good behaviors, and discouraging unwanted behaviors.

As your puppy grows and matures, his desire to chew will diminish. It is important, however, to continue giving him bones and chew toys throughout his life to exercise his jaws, keep his teeth clean, relieve boredom, release excess energy, and entertain him for a few hours.

Digging

Dogs love to dig. It's another fact of dog ownership. Some breeds dig more so than others, and their idea of fun can cause you a significant amount of frustration and heartache, especially when your precious pooch digs right under your newly planted rose bushes.

Solution

Some dogs dig holes to bury their favorite toys or bones. Others dig to find a cool spot to escape the heat. Many dogs dig out of frustration or boredom. If this is the case with your Stafford, use your imagination to come up with fun games that will stimulate his mind, burn energy, and tire him out. For example, take him for a long walk or run, play a game of retrieve, or purchase a food-dispensing puzzle that allows him to exercise his brain as he tries to outsmart the toy. Chew toys that can be stuffed with squeeze cheese or peanut butter will provide your Stafford with hours of entertainment. Or play fun find-it games in which you hide a tasty tidbit of food under a small box or bucket and encourage him to find it. You can even play hide-and-seek games, in which you encourage him to find you.

Many dogs are attracted to the smell of chicken and steer manure and love to dig and roll in fresh soil and newly fertilized gardens. The best solution for digging in gardens is prevention. Do not allow your Stafford free access to garden areas where he can dig and wreak havoc. An alternative is to install a small fence around the garden, or fence off a section of the yard just for him, where he can dig as much as he wants.

Jumping Up

Puppies and adult dogs love to jump on people. It's their way of getting close to your face and saying "Hi!" with a wet kiss. If you were to lick your friends' faces, no doubt they'd be mortified, but licking faces is a natural behavior for dogs. They don't understand that some humans take offense. Of course, if you don't mind your dog jumping on you—and some owners don't—then you have nothing to worry about. However, what you think is cute, harmless puppy behavior is far from amusing when your dog is full grown and has four muddy feet. It is equally unfair to allow him to jump on you but correct him for jumping on visitors, or to allow him to jump on you today but not tomorrow when you are wearing white pants.

Finding an Expert

If your Stafford needs specialized help, you have a number of options. Professional dog trainers and dog obedience instructors train dogs in a hands-on manner. They utilize practical methods for teaching basic obedience commands, and for reconditioning and retraining problem behaviors, such as jumping, digging, chewing, and aggression. Animal consultants and applied animal behaviorists take scientific knowledge about animal behavior and apply it to real-life situations, such as digging, chewing, separation anxiety, housetraining, and so forth. Veterinary behaviorists are medical experts with a special interest in animal behavior; they are board certified in the American Veterinary Medical Association's veterinary specialty of animal behavior. To find a behaviorist, consultant, or dog trainer, start by contacting professional organizations for a referral, such as the American College of Veterinary Behaviorists (ACVB), the American Veterinary Medical Association (AVMA), or the Animal Behavior Society (ABS). Many universities and colleges have applied animal behaviorists on staff. Contact them for referrals. Also, ask your veterinarian for a referral, because many behaviorists and trainers work with veterinarians.

Prevent jumping up by making your dog sit for a treat.

Running Away or Not Coming When Called

Staffordshire Bull Terriers who run away or refuse to come when called can create an enormous amount of frustration and angst for their owners. The good news is that this is one of the easiest problems to solve.

Solution

The key to preventing this problem is to never allow your puppy to be put in a situation in which he is allowed to develop the bad habit of running off. Each and every time you go outside,

Solution

The key is to discourage all occasions of jumping up. If you do not want your adult dog to jump on you, do not allow the behavior when he is a puppy. You can prevent jumping by making your dog sit for a kiss or cookie. Staffords are known for their superior intelligence, but even the smartest one hasn't figured out how to sit for a cookie and jump on you at the same time!

To prevent your puppy (or adult dog) from jumping on visitors, put his leash on before you open the door. This allows you to control his behavior without grabbing at his fur or collar. When he sits nicely without pawing or mauling your guests, calmly praise and reward him with a tasty tidbit.

your puppy should be on leash. If you want your puppy to run around and explore his surroundings, let him drag his leash or a lightweight long line. When he starts to wander off, simply step on the long line and reel him back in.

If your adult dog has already developed the annoying habit of running off or ignoring your *come* command, a leash or long line will prevent him from continuing to do so. Then, go back and re-teach him to come when called. Also, you should never get in the habit of chasing your puppy or allowing your kids to chase your puppy. Dogs think that this is a fun game, but it teaches them to run away from you, which is not only annoying but also dangerous. A dog who runs away from his owner can easily dart into traffic, seriously injuring himself.

Training your Stafford is an ongoing process. You must continue to reinforce positive behaviors and obedience commands—even the easy ones like *sit* and *down*—throughout his life. Not only will your Stafford enjoy spending time with you, but knowing the basic commands can help prevent problem behaviors before they start. At the very least, you will be better equipped to deal with them should they occur.

SENIOR DOG TIP

Old Dogs, New Tricks

Despite the old adage that you can't teach old dogs new tricks, senior dogs can and do learn new behaviors. It might take a bit more time and patience, but most adult dogs are willing to give it a try given the right incentive. Much depends on the age and mental status of your senior dog. A 13-year-old Stafford, for example, might have ingrained behaviors, such as urinating in the house, that are difficult (although not impossible) to fix. Rescued dogs often come with behaviors we never truly understand, such as stealing food or rummaging through the trash. First and foremost, a veterinarian should rule out any underlying medical behaviors that might be associated with an offensive behavior. And remember, offensive behaviors, such as digging and barking, are natural behaviors for a dog. Channeling that energy into positive behaviors may take the help of a qualified professional trainer. Don't give up—your adult Stafford deserves the extra attention.

Chapter 8

Stepping Out

Staffordshire Bull Terriers are smart and energetic, and they love to strut their stuff. These traits make them great candidates for a variety of canine sports and activities. Of course, you can have a great deal of fun in the process, too. National clubs and registries, such as the American Kennel Club (AKC), Kennel Club (KC) in the United Kingdom, and Staffordshire Bull Terrier Club of America (SBTCA), offer a wide variety of activities in which your Stafford can compete.

Finding the perfect sport or pastime for you and your Stafford is relatively easy because, after all, countless activities are available from which to choose. You may have to try a few different activities, but chances are there is a canine sport—or two!—with your Stafford's name on it.

Sports and Activities

Safety must always come first in any activity, especially fast-paced, high-energy activities like agility, flyball, and flying disc competitions. Before beginning any physically challenging activity, have a veterinarian examine your Stafford to rule out any joint or other medical issues. Other ways to keep your Stafford safe include:

- Dogs under the age of 2 years should never be allowed to jump. Too much pressure on developing joints can injure your puppy and lead to lifelong problems.
- When the weather is hot, confine your sports and games to the early morning or evening hours to prevent heat-related illnesses.
- Always monitor your dog for signs of fatigue and stress.
- Have plenty of water available, especially on hot days.

The following are some descriptions of sports and activities that your Stafford may enjoy.

Agility

Agility is one of the fastest growing canine sports and for good reason. Spend a few minutes watching, and you'll be hooked, too. Similar to equestrian Grand Prix courses, dogs run as fast as the wind while maneuvering through a timed obstacle course of jumps, tunnels, A-frames, weave poles, ramps, and a

Agility is a fun, fast-paced sport.

When You Can't Take Your Stafford With You

Unexpected business trips, family emergencies, and weather conditions that are too hot or too cold may exclude your best friend from your travel plans. Don't despair, however. In these situations, consider hiring a trusted friend or neighbor, boarding your Stafford, or hiring a pet sitter.

Here are some tips to help you make the best choice:

- Always tour the facility before committing. Are the kennels, runs, and exercise areas clean? Does the facility smell? Is the facility fenced? Do the kennels have good latches?
- Will your Stafford be boarded indoors or outdoors? Or both?
- Talk to the staff. Are they friendly? Experienced? Concerned about the animals?
- How much experience do they have with Staffordshire Bull Terriers?
- How frequently will your Stafford be walked or exercised? For how long? What type of exercise? Will someone interact or play with him? Or is he left unattended in an exercise yard with or without other dogs?
- What items can you bring from home? Do you need to bring his food? Blanket? Bed?

teeter-totter. Part of the lure is that it is fast-paced and exciting, and a dog gets to jump, bark, run, and strut his stuff while his owner attempts to regulate his precision.

Agility has two classes: Standard Class and Jumpers with Weaves. The Standard Class includes contact obstacles—those yellow contact zones at each end of the A-frame, dog walk, and teeter-totter. Dogs must place at least one paw in the contact zone—otherwise they receive a fault. The Jumpers with Weaves class has only jumps, tunnels, and weave poles—no contact obstacles.

Both the Standard and Jumpers class have different levels of competition: Novice, Open, and Excellent. For the die-hard competitor, the Master Agility title (MACH) is the pinnacle of agility competition.

The only drawback to this sport is that it requires a lot of equipment, which can be pretty expensive to purchase. If you are handy with a hammer and saw, you can build a lot of the equipment yourself. The best way to get started is to join a local dog-training club or visit an agility training facility.

Canine Good Citizen (CGC)

Training and interacting with your Stafford is always fun, but if organized competitions aren't your cup of tea, the

AKC's Canine Good Citizen test might be the perfect alternative. The CGC program rewards dogs who have good manners, and what's more impressive than a well-mannered Staffordshire Bull Terrier? The noncompetitive, ten-part test evaluates your Stafford's behavior in practical situations at home, in public, and in the presence of unfamiliar people and other dogs. The pass/no-pass test is designed to measure a dog's reactions to distractions, friendly strangers, and supervised isolation. Additionally, the dog must sit politely while being petted, walk on a loose leash, walk through a crowd, and respond to basic obedience commands.

Kennel clubs, trainers, and humane societies usually have information on CGC training and testing programs. Many CGC graduates go on to obedience, therapy work, or other canine sports.

Canine Freestyle

Canine freestyle allows you and your Stafford to kick up your heels, so to speak. Patterned after Olympic skating, canine freestyle is a choreographed performance between a dog and handler, set to music. It can include twists, turns, leg kicks, pivots, and other cool and creative maneuvers. Advanced competitors teach their dog to crawl, back up, wave, bow, sidestep, bounce, roll over, and so forth. The World Canine Freestyle Organization holds competitions throughout the country, and titles are awarded for high scores in technical merit and artistic impression.

Dog Shows (Conformation)

Conformation shows are the signature event of the competitive dog world, and your Staffordshire may have the goods to be a champion. Before you mail in your entry fees, let's take a look at how they work and what you must know.

For the newcomer, it often appears as if the dogs are competing against one another. And in a sense, they are. However, the judge is not comparing

Conformation judges evaluate how closely a dog measures up to the breed standard.

the quality of one Stafford against the quality of another Stafford, but rather evaluating how closely each dog measures up to the ideal Staffordshire Bull Terrier, as outlined in the breed standard. The dog who comes closest, in the judge's opinion, is the winner.

The best way to understand the conformation ring is to think of it in terms of an elimination process. Classes are divided by sex, with males and females judged separately within their breed. Male dogs are always judged first, and after being placed first through fourth, the females go through the same judging process. After the regular classes have been judged, the first-place winners of each class compete for Winners Dog and Winners Bitch. Again, males and females are judged separately, and the best male and best female receive championship points and then compete for Best of Breed. The Best of Breed winner then goes on to the Group competition. From there, he moves on to compete for the coveted and most prestigious award: Best in Show.

To get started in conformation competitions, the best thing to do is to attend a number of dog shows. Most handlers love talking shop, and they are more than happy to answer questions, provided, of course, they are not busy grooming or getting ready to go into the ring.

When Hot Is too Hot

Going places with your Stafford is always fun, be it around town or across the country, but you'll need to plan ahead during hot weather. On an 85°F (29°C) day, the temperature in a parked car, even with the all the windows partly open, can reach 102°F (39°C) in 10 minutes. Your Stafford can suffer serious brain damage or death in the time it takes you to make a quick trip into the grocery store or bank.

Flyball

Flyball is the perfect "game" for all tennis-ball loving Staffords. A high-octane relay race, flyball showcases your Stafford's speed and agility. But don't worry—your Stafford does all the running in this game. A team sport rather than an individual competition, flyball consists of four hurdles (small jumps) spaced approximately 10 feet (3 m) apart. Fifteen feet beyond the last hurdle is a spring-loaded box with a tennis ball in it. Each dog takes a turn running the relay race by leaping each of the four hurdles and then hitting a pedal or lever with his paw to trigger the box to shoot the tennis ball into the air. Once the dog catches the ball in his mouth, he races back over the

Obedience involves a retrieve exercise using dumbbells.

four hurdles to the finish line. The first team to have all four dogs run without errors wins the heat. Jump heights are determined by the height of the shortest dog on the team, which could make your Stafford quite the valuable teammate!

Obedience Trials

Obedience trials go well beyond the CGC requirements, and if you love training your Stafford, obedience competitions may be your cup of tea. Obedience trials require your Stafford to perform a number of specific exercises that showcase his training and how well he obeys your commands. Dogs can compete in three different levels: Novice, Open, and Utility, with each level becoming increasingly more difficult. The novice class, for example, includes heeling on and off leash, coming when called,

a stand for examination, and a *sit-stay* and *down-stay*. The advanced classes include jumping, hand signals, retrieving, and scent discrimination.

A perfect score is 200. A qualifying score is 170, and dogs must earn at least half of the possible points in each exercise. A dog who receives a qualifying score earns a leg toward his title in that particular level. When he earns three legs, he earns an obedience title. Dogs must earn a title in the lower-level classes before moving on to the next level.

Rally Obedience

Rally obedience was created with the average dog owner in mind. Less formal and rigorous than traditional obedience trials, dog and handler proceed at their own pace through a course of designated stations. Each station has a sign providing instructions regarding the skill that is to be performed, such as Halt & Sit, Right Turn, About Right Turn, and so forth.

Dogs and handlers can compete in three levels: Novice, Advanced, and Excellent. Like traditional obedience, each level becomes increasingly more demanding, and dogs and handlers must receive three qualifying scores in each level before progressing to the next level. Dogs who earn at least 70 points out of a possible 100 are awarded a leg. Three legs are required for a rally obedience title.

Tracking

Designed to test a Stafford's ability to recognize and track a human scent over varying terrains and climatic changes, you can teach your Stafford to track for fun, such as finding his toys or a treat that you have hidden in the house or yard, or you can teach him to track as a sport. The AKC offers three tracking titles: Tracking Dog (TD), Tracking Dog Excellent (TDX), and Variable Surface Tracking (VST). If a Stafford successfully completes all three tracking

titles, he earns the prestigious title of Champion Tracker (CT).

Tracking tests vary by tracking distance, length of time the scent was laid, and physical surfaces. However, the primary goal is for the dog to follow a scented track and locate an article left at the end of the trail by a tracklayer. Unlike obedience and agility titles that require a dog and handler to qualify three times, a Stafford only needs to complete one track successfully to earn each title.

The AKC can provide more information about these fun and challenging competitions.

Weight Pulling

Weight-pulling competitions are similar to tractor-pulling competitions—except your Stafford does all the work! Dogs, who must be at least 2 years of age, compete within their individual weight class to see who can pull the most weight over 16 feet (4.9 m). A dog can pull a weighted sled on snow or a wheeled cart on a natural surface. Specially designed harnesses disperse tension and reduce the possibility of injury. The weight is gradually increased until one dog remains. The AKC

It's important to keep your Stafford hydrated while he's exercising or competing.

Your well-mannered Stafford might make an excellent therapy dog.

requirement, it does help if your Stafford is certified for therapy work. At the minimum, your dog must be obedience trained and in possession of a Canine Good Citizen certificate.

does not sanction weight-pulling competitions; however, information is available through a number of clubs, including the United Kennel Club (UKC) and the International Weight Pull Association (IWPA).

Service Opportunities

Did you know that well-mannered Staffordshire Bull Terriers can and do make wonderful therapy dogs by providing unconditional love, companionship, and emotional support to nursing-home, hospital, assisted-living, and mental-health residents? Owners volunteering with their Staffords make regularly scheduled visits and brighten the lives of residents by providing stimulation, companionship, and a vehicle for conversation and interaction. Staffords must be well mannered and have a sound temperament. While not a

FAMILY-FRIENDLY TIP

Traveling With Kids and Your Stafford

Staffords make excellent traveling companions. You can make the trip more enjoyable by incorporating your children in the daily traveling chores. For example, have them keep track of the sun so that it isn't beating through the window on your dog, causing him to overheat. Let them track scheduled breaks, and sound the alarm when it's time for a pit stop. Older children can help clean up any pit stop messes and make sure that the dog gets enough water. Traveling with your four-legged friend takes planning and a good deal of patience, but with a bit of organization, there's no reason your precious pooch can't come along, too.

Travel

Staffords love a good road trip, and although most are quite adaptable and make wonderful travelers, don't wait until you are on the road to discover that yours is not! Ideally, it is best to accustom your Stafford to traveling while he is young and more receptive to new adventures. If you have an older Stafford, don't despair. With a bit of patience, he too can learn to love road trips, whether they are across town or across the country.

It's safer for your Stafford to travel in a crate rather than loose in the front seat.

When traveling, don't forget to pack a few necessities for your Stafford. In addition to his crate, collar, and leash, be sure to include these must-have items:

- enough food and bottled water to last for the journey—and perhaps a day or two longer in case of unexpected delays
- current health certificate and rabies inoculation
- current photographs, to be used for ID should he become lost
- pooper-scooper, paper towels, or plastic bags for picking up after your dog
- first-aid kit and any medications or prescriptions, if necessary
- chew toys, bones, tug toys, balls, and the like
- a favorite blanket or bed
- an adequate supply of doggy towels for quick cleanups, in the event your dog gets wet, dirty, or injured

Car Rides

Weather permitting, your Stafford is sure to enjoy short trips to the market, bank, and so forth. Young puppies and adult dogs should ride in their crate to curtail any vomiting or potty accidents and to prevent them from distracting you, gnawing on the leather seats,

Traveling With Senior Staffords

As your Stafford ages, he will no doubt continue to enjoy road trips, but you will need to take extra precautions to ensure his safety and comfort.

- Before traveling, consult your veterinarian. Make sure that your dog is healthy, fully vaccinated, and up for the journey.

- Older dogs move more slowly, so be patient.

- Pack any medications your Stafford takes regularly, including pain medications.

- Take along his favorite bed or blanket so that he can enjoy the comforts of home while on the road.

- Strange places can confuse and disorient an older dog, so be extra patient, keep him close, and reassure him that you are nearby.

- Keep a close eye on his health. Be sure that he is eating and drinking daily.

102

Staffordshire Bull Terriers

eating your cell phone, or ransacking the groceries. If you should stop suddenly or get in an accident, your Stafford will be safer when confined in his crate. He should also be wearing his buckle collar with ID tag. If your errands take you away from home for more than an hour or so, carry bottled water in case he gets thirsty and paper bags for cleaning up after him should a pit stop be necessary.

Longer trips, be they across the state or across the country, require a bit more planning, but they can be equally pleasurable for both you and your dog. If your Stafford is used to riding in the car, longer trips should not present too many problems. You will need to stop every few hours to let your dog relieve himself and burn off some pent-up energy. Unless your Stafford is a seasoned traveler, it is best to limit his food intake 2 hours before traveling. Feed the bulk of his food after you have stopped for the day. Talk to your veterinarian about any additional vaccinations or medications that your Stafford might need, depending on your destination.

Flying the Friendly Skies

Airplane journeys require quite a bit more planning, but they are well worth the effort if your Stafford enjoys being with you. Dogs traveling by air are protected by US Department of Agriculture (USDA) regulations; this means that they must be at least 8 weeks old and travel in airline-approved crates. Not all airlines accept dogs, and many limit the number

Your well-behaved Stafford should be able to accompany you to many places.

of dogs accepted on each flight, so planning ahead is essential. Your Stafford will need specific types of documentation, including a health certificate issued by a veterinarian within 10 days of travel. Dogs traveling outside the continental United States may be subjected to quarantine regulations.

Notify the airlines that your Stafford is traveling with you. Puppies and pint-sized dogs can ride in the cabin, but most likely your Stafford will travel in the cargo hold area. Therefore, when scheduling flights, try to book nonstop flights during the middle of the week, avoiding holiday or weekend travel. Avoid layovers and plane changes, if possible. During warm weather, choose flights early in the morning or late in the evening, and in cooler months, choose midday flights.

Accommodations

If your travels with your Stafford include staying at a hotel, motel, or campground, call ahead to be sure that they accept dogs. Not everyone accepts dogs—even well-behaved Staffordshire Bull Terriers. Some facilities allow dogs in the rooms but may require the dog to be crated. Some larger hotels provide kennel facilities; many require a refundable pet deposit or nonrefundable pet fee.

Staffords are pretty adaptable, and most likely yours won't care where you go or what you do as long as he's included in your plans and can spend time with you.

Resources

Associations and Organizations

Breed Clubs

American Kennel Club (AKC)
5580 Centerview Drive
Raleigh, NC 27606
Telephone: (919) 233-9767
Fax: (919) 233-3627
E-mail: info@akc.org
www.akc.org

Canadian Kennel Club (CKC)
89 Skyway Avenue, Suite 100
Etobicoke, Ontario M9W 6R4
Telephone: (416) 675-5511
Fax: (416) 675-6506
E-mail: information@ckc.ca
www.ckc.ca

Federation Cynologique Internationale (FCI)
Secretariat General de la FCI
Place Albert 1er, 13
B – 6530 Thuin
Belqique
www.fci.be

The Kennel Club
1 Clarges Street
London
W1J 8AB
Telephone: 0870 606 6750
Fax: 0207 518 1058
www.the-kennel-club.org.uk

United Kennel Club (UKC)
100 E. Kilgore Road
Kalamazoo, MI 49002-5584
Telephone: (269) 343-9020
Fax: (269) 343-7037
E-mail: pbickell@ukcdogs.com
www.ukcdogs.com

Pet Sitters

National Association of Professional Pet Sitters
15000 Commerce Parkway, Suite C
Mt. Laurel, New Jersey 08054
Telephone: (856) 439-0324
Fax: (856) 439-0525
E-mail: napps@ahint.com
www.petsitters.org

Pet Sitters International
201 East King Street
King, NC 27021-9161
Telephone: (336) 983-9222
Fax: (336) 983-5266
E-mail: info@petsit.com
www.petsit.com

Rescue Organizations and Animal Welfare Groups

American Humane Association (AHA)
63 Inverness Drive East
Englewood, CO 80112
Telephone: (303) 792-9900
Fax: 792-5333
www.americanhumane.org

American Society for the Prevention of Cruelty to Animals (ASPCA)
424 E. 92nd Street
New York, NY 10128-6804
Telephone: (212) 876-7700
www.aspca.org

Royal Society for the Prevention of Cruelty to Animals (RSPCA)
Telephone: 0870 3335 999
Fax: 0870 7530 284
www.rspca.org.uk

The Humane Society of the United States (HSUS)
2100 L Street, NW
Washington DC 20037
Telephone: (202) 452-1100
www.hsus.org

Sports

Canine Freestyle Federation, Inc.
Secretary: Brandy Clymire
E-Mail: secretary@canine-freestyle.org
www.canine-freestyle.org

International Agility Link (IAL)
Global Administrator: Steve Drinkwater
E-mail: yunde@powerup.au
www.agilityclick.com/~ial

North American Dog Agility Council
11522 South Hwy 3
Cataldo, ID 83810
www.nadac.com

North American Flyball Association
www.flyball.org
1400 West Devon Avenue #512
Chicago, IL 6066
800-318-6312

United States Dog Agility Association
P.O. Box 850955
Richardson, TX 75085-0955
Telephone: (972) 487-2200
www.usdaa.com

World Canine Freestyle Organization
P.O. Box 350122
Brooklyn, NY 11235-2525
Telephone: (718) 332-8336
www.worldcaninefreestyle.org

Therapy

Delta Society
875 124th Ave NE, Suite 101
Bellevue, WA 98005
Telephone: (425) 226-7357
Fax: (425) 235-1076
E-mail: info@deltasociety.org
www.deltasociety.org

Therapy Dogs Incorporated
PO Box 5868
Cheyenne, WY 82003
Telephone: (877) 843-7364
E-mail: therdog@sisna.com
www.therapydogs.com

Therapy Dogs International (TDI)
88 Bartley Road
Flanders, NJ 07836
Telephone: (973) 252-9800
Fax: (973) 252-7171
E-mail: tdi@gti.net
www.tdi-dog.org

Training

Association of Pet Dog Trainers (APDT)
150 Executive Center Drive Box 35
Greenville, SC 29615
Telephone: (800) PET-DOGS
Fax: (864) 331-0767
E-mail: information@apdt.com
www.apdt.com

National Association of Dog Obedience Instructors (NADOI)
PMB 369
729 Grapevine Hwy.
Hurst, TX 76054-2085
www.nadoi.org

Veterinary and Health Resources

Academy of Veterinary Homeopathy (AVH)
P.O. Box 9280
Wilmington, DE 19809
Telephone: (866) 652-1590
Fax: (866) 652-1590
E-mail: office@TheAVH.org
www.theavh.org

American Academy of Veterinary Acupuncture (AAVA)
100 Roscommon Drive, Suite 320
Middletown, CT 06457
Telephone: (860) 635-6300
Fax: (860) 635-6400
E-mail: office@aava.org
www.aava.org

American Animal Hospital Association (AAHA)
P.O. Box 150899
Denver, CO 80215-0899
Telephone: (303) 986-2800
Fax: (303) 986-1700
E-mail: info@aahanet.org
www.aahanet.org/index.cfm

American College of Veterinary Internal Medicine (ACVIM)
1997 Wadsworth Blvd., Suite A
Lakewood, CO 80214-5293
Telephone: (800) 245-9081
Fax: (303) 231-0880
Email: ACVIM@ACVIM.org
www.acvim.org

American College of Veterinary Ophthalmologists (ACVO)
P.O. Box 1311
Meridian, Idaho 83860
Telephone: (208) 466-7624
Fax: (208) 466-7693
E-mail: office@acvo.com
www.acvo.com

American Holistic Veterinary Medical Association (AHVMA)
2218 Old Emmorton Road
Bel Air, MD 21015
Telephone: (410) 569-0795
Fax: (410) 569-2346
E-mail: office@ahvma.org
www.ahvma.org

American Veterinary Medical Association (AVMA)
1931 North Meacham Road – Suite 100
Schaumburg, IL 60173
Telephone: (847) 925-8070

Fax: (847) 925-1329
E-mail: avmainfo@avma.org
www.avma.org

ASPCA Animal Poison Control Center
1717 South Philo Road, Suite 36
Urbana, IL 61802
Telephone: (888) 426-4435
www.aspca.org

British Veterinary Association (BVA)
7 Mansfield Street
London
W1G 9NQ
Telephone: 020 7636 6541
Fax: 020 7436 2970
E-mail: bvahq@bva.co.uk
www.bva.co.uk

Canine Eye Registration Foundation (CERF)
VMDB/CERF
1248 Lynn Hall
625 Harrison St.
Purdue University
West Lafayette, IN 47907-2026
Telephone: (765) 494-8179
E-mail: CERF@vmbd.org
www.vmdb.org

Orthopedic Foundation for Animals (OFA)
2300 NE Nifong Blvd
Columbus, Missouri 65201-3856
Telephone: (573) 442-0418
Fax: (573) 875-5073
Email: ofa@offa.org
www.offa.org

Publications

Books
Anderson, Teoti. *The Super Simple Guide to Housetraining*. Neptune City: TFH Publications, 2004.

Morgan, Diane. *Good Dogkeeping*. Neptune City: TFH Publications, 2005.

Magazines
AKC *Family Dog*
American Kennel Club
260 Madison Avenue
New York, NY 10016
Telephone: (800) 490-5675
E-mail: familydog@akc.org
www.akc.org/pubs/familydog

AKC *Gazette*
American Kennel Club
260 Madison Avenue
New York, NY 10016
Telephone: (800) 533-7323
E-mail: gazette@akc.org
www.akc.org/pubs/gazette

Dog & Kennel
Pet Publishing, Inc.
7-L Dundas Circle
Greensboro, NC 27407
Telephone: (336) 292-4272
Fax: (336) 292-4272
E-mail: info@petpublishing.com
www.dogandkennel.com

Resources

Index

Note: Boldfaced numbers indicate illustrations.

About the Author

Tracy Libby is an award-winning freelance writer and coauthor of *Building Blocks for Performance* (Alpine 2002), as well as five books for T.F.H. Publications, Inc. Her articles have appeared in numerous publications, including the *AKC Gazette, Puppies USA, You and Your Dog,* and *Dog Fancy's Popular Dogs* series. She is a member of the Dog Writers Association of America and a recipient of the Ellsworth S. Howell award for distinguished dog writing. She has been involved in the sport of dogs for 20 years, exhibiting in conformation and obedience.

Photo Credits

REACH OUT. ACT. RESPOND.

Go to AnimalPlanet.com/ROAR and find out how you can be a voice for animals everywhere!